SURRENDERING TO
MARRIAGE

SURRENDERING TO
MARRIAGE

Husbands, Wives, and Other Imperfections

IRIS KRASNOW

talk miramax books

HYPERION

NEW YORK

Library of Congress Cataloging-in-Publication Data

ISBN: 9-7868-6218-1 (hardcover)
ISBN 0-7868-8771-0 (paperback)

FIRST PAPERBACK EDITION

10   9   8   7   6   5   4   3   2   1

To Chuck,
my husband

Acknowledgments

First off, I'd like to thank Jonathan Burnham, president and editor-in-chief of Talk Miramax Books, for pushing me to write a book on marriage when I absolutely did not want to write a book about marriage. In fact, at the time of our exploratory conversation in early 1998, I didn't even want to be married.

Jonathan assured me that pain was wonderful fuel for a writer, and after listening to much cajoling in his irresistible British accent, I said, "Okay, but the only way I can do this book is if I approach it is as if I were a foreign correspondent dispatched to a strange country, like I had just been dropped into Bangladesh." Of course, once I got into the subject, it was impossible to look at marriage with a detached journalist's eye, at arm's length, like it was they, not me, with all the problems. *Surrendering to Marriage* immediately became an us book, as people dissected their own relationships and forced me to examine the one I was, and still am, in.

Also at that table that fateful day was my longtime editor Susan Dalsimer, my patient guide on this project, a woman who also coached me through *Surrendering to Motherhood*. A woman with a big heart, she made me give this book my whole heart. I thank you for everything.

Susan Mercandetti, acquisitions editor of Talk/Miramax, also gets an enormous thank you, for being my tough-love critic. Susan sharpened my focus and kept me laughing and moving through the countless drafts when I felt like I couldn't write one more word.

I am also enormously appreciative of my editor in the Style section of the *Washington Post*, Peggy Hackman. I've been writing for Peggy for fifteen years. She has always given me two cherished gifts—freedom, and reins.

I'm a low-tech writer, who came of age on an IBM Selectric, and I couldn't have gotten any of these words from my computer in Maryland to my publisher in New York City without my high-tech sorceress Laura Hollon. Laura's mastery of computers helped me out of every jam I got in with my iMac, of which there were many. Laura, you are my savior!

To my assistant, Betsy Doughty, I offer profound gratitude as well. Over the months of research, Betsy devoured piles of books and magazines, to extract quotes and examples for this book on surrendering to long-term commitment. As I interviewed dozens of other people, it was Betsy who sat down with me at my kitchen table, turned a tape recorder on, and interviewed me, excavating much of the first-person narrative you will see. She is an amazing and loyal friend.

Amazing and loyal siblings and friends kept me going every step of the way. There is no way to write about marriage unless you've got smart and funny comrades who are willing to dish about marriage. When I wanted to stop writing they told me, "Keep going, you can do it." Thank you, Greg Krasnow and Fran Krasnow, my brother and sister, for listening to me and loving me all these years. Thank you, Moe Hanson, my comrade and confidante who has shared many a conversation and many a bottle of wine during this process. I'd also like to thank my treasured circle of longtime girlfriends, whose compassion and empathy bolstered me to the finish line: Randi Altschuler, Marcy Curland, Ellyn Dooley, Simone Gould, Sarah Haskell, Joanie Haskell, Diana McLellan, Terri Rubin, Amy Rudnick, Gail Watkins, and Debbie Wolman. (You are listed in alphabetical order, not in the order in which I cherish you.) And thank you, raucous Ladies of the Club, the members of our thirteen-year-old book club who, unfailingly, are my most devoted cheerleaders.

May I also thank here three women I admire who have shown me through their own marriages what a good relationship should look like—Karen White, Shereen El-Said and Florence Wiedemann. Every woman needs a couple of close guy friends as well, and I have two of the best. These men I adore have gratefully helped me get clearer about how to interpret behaviors native to the male species, Tom Ferraro and Harry Jaffe.

Two tenacious college students are also deeply appreciated. Winston Beigel and Colin Degan pored through books and Internet dispatches for anecdotes that portrayed the changing face of marriage. Constructing a book requires many levels of masonry, and I would also like to thank Kristin Powers at Talk Miramax Books for her role in overseeing the actual building of the book.

Above all, I'd like to thank my husband, Chuck Anthony, and our sons, Theodore, Isaac, Jackson, and Zane. They show me each day, in huge and small ways, why working on my marriage should be a sacred and unrelenting effort. And to my parents, Helene and Theodore Krasnow, I can never thank you enough for staying married. Coming from a home where my mother and father both lived together has given me two crucial traits, strength and optimism. Although my father died in 1986, his grand spirit and humor are with me forever.

My literary agent, Jan Miller, is a woman of great instinct and great energy, and I am blessed to have her by my side. And to Ruth Berlin, thank you for keeping us focused on the light. Finally, to the generous people who tell their stories in *Surrendering to Marriage,* I have shielded your identity but your startling honesty about your own husbands and wives form the true spine of this book. To you, I owe everything.

SURRENDERING TO
MARRIAGE

PROLOGUE

*Staying married and staying humble is a path
to spiritual and psychic wholeness.*

When I teach my journalism students at American University about the art of feature and profile writing, I talk about excavating the human spirit with a graceful, compassionate, but relentless line of questioning. We often discussed my own interviews for this book, which in twenty-two years as a journalist have been my most difficult excavation. Sit down with anyone who has been married for a while, and if he or she is genuinely honest, there are wrenching stories to be unearthed. Excavating my own memories of a twelve-year rocking and rolling marriage has been painful in itself, reflecting on the numerous times I've wanted to bolt and why instead I've stayed with Chuck, my imperfect husband who is the father of our four perfect sons.

This book should have been published a year ago, but it was a stop and start process. Just when I'd be forging ahead, some marital tiff would knock me off course. I'd call my editor, Susan Dalsimer, and tell her I couldn't write about marriage because I was so consumed by my own challenging marriage and she always said the same thing: "That's great! Write it. It's what many people are feeling but cannot express." And so I have written it, what goes on in a real marriage, with too many disappointments, too much grinding reality, too little time. I've written about the fine line that divides love and hate, about temptation, and about midlife malaise. And I've written about the profound joy that can be ours if we surrender to marriage as a commitment we made, a spiritual promise larger than our own selfish desires.

Illustrated with story after story from people in all stages of marriage—infatuation to boredom to philandering to divorce—this book is filled with ways to work a marriage, and reasons why we have to keep up the work, even when it hurts. It's a book about being reborn in something old, about believing in the eternal light that awaits us at the end of all the tunnels we will hit. I am ecstatic to be writing this first-appearing but last-written prologue of my book; it's like framing a painting I never thought would be done.

During the nearly three years it took to compose *Surrendering to Marriage*, my own marriage got better; I mean *really* better. The content of my relationship with Chuck did not change. We still have an imperfect marriage. But my attitude changed—dramatically. I now accept and expect imperfection. I expect that we will fight and that we will make up, make love and that we will fight again. Friction used to make me want to flee; I still don't like it but it is what it is, and to expect two opposite personalities, of different genders, to live without clashes in one house forever is ludicrous. Deciding that the promise I made at my wedding, "Until death do us part," was not just some line from a movie, strange things started happening. I began to relax, and our disagreements are less hostile, more like we are chest-pounding apes in the jungle going through theatrics than a husband and wife truly on the brink of splitting.

Yet, my fantasy of marriage as a wellspring of contentment has completely disappeared, and so should yours. Thinking you get happiness ever after is a ticket to divorce. I'll tell you the four things I now know about marriage, from my own transforming relationship and from conversations with other flummoxed spouses: A. Marriage can be hell; B. The grass is not greener on the other side; C. Savor the highs, because one thing you can count on—the dips are just around the corner; and D. Nobody is perfect, so you may as well love the one you're with.

To get to this stage took a lot of work and a lot of tears. I cannot imagine going through this psyche-searing task again with someone new. Therefore, I surrender to this imperfect marriage, because I love it more than I hate it and I committed to this man with a promise that I need to, we all need to, do our best to fulfill.

These are not all romantic truths, but this is the truth, so get it and get on with things. "Love the one you're with" is particularly significant; it means if you are searching for perfect love elsewhere, this book can save you a lot of heartache by showing you that no such animal exists. Listen to some of the following stories, and you will hear that what you often get with someone you believed to be smarter and sexier are even bigger problems than the ones you left behind. This from dealing with stepchildren, ex-spouses, and the realization that the same tough issues are surfacing again, because you took your own imperfect self with you, and from that there is no escape.

I am not unequivocally anti-divorce. There are many couples that have broken up for valid reasons—abuse, abandonment, addictions, intolerable loneliness. But I am unequivocally promarriage, and my hope is that this book helps those couples headed for separation to look hard at what they are leaving and whether they are headed to a healthier place.

My hope is that if couples have even a shard of love left between them that they will try to build upon that sliver and
work on constructing an indestructible partnership. It takes
tenacity, tolerance, and time. Divorce is rarely a solution to
misery, as the bruised people on these pages will tell you.

My attorney sister, Fran Krasnow, who specializes in family law, in Chicago, hears about the suffering and wreckage of
divorce in her work every day. As she advises, "If there is a
glimmer of hope left that a marriage will survive, I strongly
recommend that the couple seeks counseling. They can always
get divorced later if that's the only option.

"Couples are much less likely to reconcile after they have
gone through the acrimony of a divorce. The work on a marriage needs to be done *while* you're married."

A college administrator who recently left the father of her
three young children because she fell madly in love with someone else puts it this way: "I am crazy about this new man, but
I can tell anyone in the same situation that leaving a marriage
is living hell. Your children are going to be screwed up. Mine
are not eating or sleeping well. My ex-husband says mean
things about me to the kids, which is terrible for them. It has
been devastating, to all of us. If there is any possible way you
can repair your marriage, do it."

This woman friend of twenty years and my sister have
taught me to keep repairing and repairing. We all hear stories
about the agony that comes from separating families, shuffling
children with suitcases between two houses, and the Revenge
of the Spouse, which can go on forever. The times I've wanted
to leave, my compulsion to live apart from Chuck has always
been far weaker than the prospect of living even one day apart
from my children. I have found that if I wait the squalls of
marriage out, they always pass, and a softer wind blows
through that makes me feel as if I'm the luckiest woman

alive, to be with a partner who is fiercely devoted to me and our boys.

Marriage is not a bad thing—I used to think it was. Marriage is a good thing, of this I am increasingly convinced. I am now as certain as any mortal can be about anything that I am going to stay married, come "hell or high water," like my dear friend Patty Hutchens, a Presbyterian minister's wife married for forty years, likes to say. Perhaps you'll be left with the same fixed mind-set when you read in *Surrendering to Marriage* what others have to say about hating marriage but staying married and finding out that their relationship isn't so miserable after all. When we alter our expectations, satisfaction can be abundant. I'll tell you one thing that needs to be altered about expectations in relationships: that someone else can make us happy. An intrinsically unhappy person who leaves one marriage is going to be an unhappy person in a second and third marriage. Happiness is self-generated.

As I am writing this, a new *Time* magazine is lying on the floor of my office, picturing a child on the cover with a bleak expression, her little face resting in her hands. In back of her, her father and mother are standing apart. The headline reads: "What Divorce Does to Kids: New Research Says the Long-term Damage is Worse Than You Thought." Inside is an article prompted by Judith Wallerstein's new book, *The Unexpected Legacy of Divorce*, which cites testimony from young adults that their parents' divorces have left them with serious and lasting traumas, among them a profound expectation of failure in their own marriages and an overall sense of uncertainty about life itself.

The best we can do for our children, and for ourselves, is to make our own marriages go the distance, weathering waves of sadness, even rage, because we know that our grit and perseverance are going to pay off hugely in the end. In *Surrendering to Marriage* are voices of senior citizens who say they are more in love than ever with the partner they married a half-century ago. It is not a love of lust and infatuation. It is the deepest of love, built over time, through joy and tragedy.

Marriage is not designed to make us happy; it is God's way of forcing us to grow into responsible adults.

My dream is that when our own four sons, now ages six through ten, are choosing wives two decades from now, their view of marriage will be as a lifelong adventure, and that the darkness of the divorce era will seem like ancient history. We, the restless baby boomers, can use the wisdom from our own mistakes to become leaders of a marriage renaissance, and put all this silliness behind us. Most husbands and wives, even the ones who hate as much as they love, can survive as a couple if they lighten up and surrender. I could have left Chuck a thousand times throughout our marriage. After writing this book, I am relieved to still be his wife, because I now know, and you are about to, what lies on the other side of the fence.

Surrendering to Marriage is a three-part voyage. On the first stop, I take you into the thick of "The Malaise," that simmering, lingering dissatisfaction that makes lots of people question their marriages and fantasize about a more enticing mate, a more exciting life. The second destination is called "The Choice," a place where spouses speak out on the decision to leave a marriage when the malaise became too great, or when they found love and romance elsewhere. In this section, there are also stories from people who stayed with partners after their affairs were discovered, using the pain to transform their wobbly marriages into sturdier, more honest unions. Lastly, you will land in "The Surrender," the final lap of the book packed with people and reasons that demonstrate why staying married, and staying humble, is a path to psychic and spiritual wholeness.

All the characters in this book and their stories are real, but some names and identifying details have been changed.

My sources who wanted to remain anonymous were asked to pick their own pseudonyms; some asked that no name be used at all.

May this journey into the soul of marriage—with all its foibles and imperfections—take you to a higher place in your own relationship.

The Malaise

We share neither blood nor genes, perhaps not even common
interests. Yet we met and married and now share
a home, in-laws, and children.
It can be hell.

I am forty-five and could live another fifty-five years. My vision of that life is with my husband Chuck at my side, in this house of weathered shingles on a hill near the Chesapeake Bay. We've been married twelve years, which already seems like a century—what's another few decades? During the three years of research for this book, I've scrutinized my marriage and dissected dozens of other marriages, and the process has been both enlightening and excruciating. Because marriage itself is brutal some days, challenging most days, rarely easy.

My women friends have said many things to me over the years when I've thrashed around in my marriage: "Nothing is perfect," or "Maybe you married the wrong person," or "You're not trying hard enough." And I've returned similar comments when they've shared their own marital malaise. Relationships between spouses are impossible to understand or explain, yet one thing is clear and certain: Our girlfriends are the ones who keep us going when we feel like our men aren't coming through for us.

Here's what I've learned after twelve years with Chuck, a smart and sexy and imperfect man who is the father of our four perfect sons: I did not marry the wrong person; there's plenty of hate that comes with love; and although I wish I didn't have to try so hard to make marriage work, I know that

I do. Everybody does. If they say they don't, they are either lying, or never see their spouses.

Marriage is difficult and mysterious, but essential. Indeed, a good marriage means a good life. This book is about staying married, and how to transcend the ambiguity and temptation caused by midlife malaise. Thus the choice of title, *Surrendering to Marriage*, a yielding to a spiritual force greater than ourselves. This is not surrendering as in cowering in submission to another's will, as preached in this passage from Ephesians: "Wives, submit to your husbands as to the Lord. For the husband is the head of the wife as Christ is the head of the church. . . . Now as the church submits to Christ, so also wives should submit to their husbands in everything."

Surrendering means submitting to your own integrity, to your wedding promise, for the duration. This in the face of the fantasies, boredom, and darkness that arise in long-term relationships. This in the face of the statistics of doom that have hovered over American couples for the past thirty years—half of marriages end in divorce.

We, the members of the baby boom, have found thus far the notion of traditional marriage as the ticket to eternal fulfillment tough to swallow after spending our growing-up years moving on to the Next Big Thing, from sex, bongs, and the Grateful Dead to sex, Prozac, and a misguided obsession with staying young. Making it to the twenty-five-year anniversary mark and beyond requires relinquishing our cravings for novelty and ego gratification—no simple feat for the generation with the longstanding mantra "Me, me, me, me." We are the dreamy believers in author Tom Robbins's tantalizing promise: "It's never too late to have a happy childhood."

In my first book, *Surrendering to Motherhood*, I spoke of the surrender that comes from sublimating personal desires and yielding to the higher power of raising children. Yet, as challenging as the shift into parenting can be, it is effortless compared to the concessions and compromises that must take place in marriage. Our love for our children is uncomplicated and spontaneous, pure and immense. Our children whom we bore, and who resemble us in body and face, are natural extensions of ourselves, like our legs. We love them without condition, without doubt, without any brain games.

In marriage, no matter how deep the love and devotion, our partner is still The Other, someone we may think we know very, very well, but who is always somewhat of a stranger. We share neither blood nor genes, perhaps not even common interests. Yet we met and married and now share a home, in-laws, and children.

It can be hell.

Surrendering to marriage means realizing that to succeed in this most mysterious and difficult, yet essential, of partnerships we must push through waves of sadness and rage, and accept them as part of the whole marriage organism that also includes the profound joy of being in a committed union, and of giving your kids a rock to hold onto.

Surrendering to marriage means we must be forgiving and flexible when what we really feel like doing is spewing venomous remarks. We must give back rubs or our bodies when we feel like reading or sleeping. We must keep our marriages alive, and revive them when they are dying.

We must surrender to reality and let go of fantasy.

Ultimately, surrendering to marriage, if it's with a spouse who isn't destroying us with hands or words or by total apathy, means coming to know there is nothing better out there because wherever we go we still have ourselves to lug along. People who leave a marriage for someone else often end up finding that person carries heavier baggage than the partner they left behind. Without the old, imperfect partner around to blame anymore we find it was our imperfect self that was the cause of our own pain all along.

I come to my conclusions not as an academic or psychologist with far-flung, longitudinal studies to prove my theories. I come as a nosy journalist who has asked lots of people lots of embarrassing questions—in kitchens, in restaurants, on airplanes, on walks along beaches, on the telephone, in emails. There are all sorts of men and women represented, from all pockets of the country, all income levels, all cultural backgrounds. Yet, much of the best stuff in here comes from the anguished voices in my own backyard, that is, an extended circle of friends around Washington, D.C., journalists, artists, nurses, doctors, lawyers, waitresses, heiresses.

I did not try to air male and female perspectives equally; you will hear voices from husbands, but this is predominantly a woman's take, from a mother and wife whose own chameleonesque marriage is the central journey of this book.

And what my own raw data tells me, from the generous people who allowed me to root around in their hearts, and from probing my own mercurial feelings about marriage, is that no relationship can fix our woes and finally give us the happiness that has thus far eluded us. Smitten men and women who appear superhumanly heroic to each other during courtship evolve into naked and annoying husbands and wives. Women who wear red Victoria's Secret panties during courtship put on beige Sears cotton underwear during marriage. Hard-bodied male suitors become potbellied husbands.

I'm in my kitchen slapping together lunches, arranging them neatly in L.L. Bean thermal packs, and thinking of roads not taken, possibilities unfulfilled. I should be thinking how wonderful it is to be making four peanut butter and honey sandwiches for four adorable sons, but instead here's what's running through my mind: If I have to make one more sandwich I'm going to lose my mind.

Running a household is the same every day. We are machines going through repetitive tasks, too often unconscious to the flow of the motion or the pulse of the moment. No matter how helpful a husband is, women generally end up being Command Central, in charge of overseeing the whole of the operation and attending to the myriad of details, the buying, scheduling, organizing, most of the cleaning and cooking. The Buddhists tell us to be fully awake in the here and now. "Just be with it because it is there, like the wind, the cicadas, the cool rain . . . ," Toni Packer advises us in in her book *The Work of This Moment*. Ah, if it were only that easy, to swirl like the wind, to fall effortlessly like the rain, to become the motion while doing mundane chores at home after dropping kids off at school or returning from the office, and not let embittered thoughts about monotony fling us into a reverie about a more enticing future.

Even when we try hard to embrace each moment, days with children who need rides everywhere—this while handling our professions—get hammered into clumps of anonymous weeks that blur into anonymous months. As the routine goes: Get up, get dressed, get kids dressed, feed them breakfast, clean up after breakfast, take them to school, shove in as much work of your own as you possibly can the hours they are away, pick them up, take them to soccer, piano, orthodontist, come home, make dinner, scoop up food off the floor, homework, baths, bedtime, then come downstairs to your clean kitchen to make it dirty again when you start all over making school lunches for the following day.

It's hardly shocking that people often seek an escape from the grind in the form of illicit love with fetching strangers. We are, after all, the generation who grew up in dread of stopping too long in any one place as not to miss the higher-intensity drama we are certain awaits us around the next corner, through the next door, with the next mate. Yet, while the real guys we married may be flawed, at least they are people whose imperfections we are used to. At least they are men we can count on, men we loved once, may still love, and if we don't now, will love again. At least they are husbands who will stay home and baby-sit when we can't stand it anymore and need to run away from home for a few hours to have martinis with girlfriends.

It's easy to fall for charming seducers who keep you hanging with promises to free you from the chains of the mundane. But these suitors are fairy-tale characters until they withstand the reality test of the twenty-four-hour life cycle. Before you ditch your own boring spouse, put Mr. Happily Ever After to this test—get fat, don't shave, be bitchy, and bring a snot-nosed, whiny child on one of your lunch dates. In other words, be real around them, and see how it transforms your idealized-perfect-soul-mate love. I'll take an imperfect marriage I can touch and feel over an unproven Mr. Right who is perfect only in my dreams.

Every Sunday morning when I go out for bagels, I am reminded of how nearly perfect my husband actually is. There is one divorced father who I always see at the bakery, a stubby man in white shorts and Italian loafers who drives a white Jeep with gold detailing. He has year-round orange skin from the tanning salon, his upper arms are gross bulges from his routines at Gold's Gym. He talks to me, he talks to all the women, not meeting us at eye level, but zooming in at boob level. You know the type—leering, salivating, the kind of guy who makes your husband in the flannel shirt and old jeans seem like the most spectacular male alive. There are lots of Orange Men out there, I remind myself, making what's in here, this man in my house, so much more appreciated.

Yet, these feelings of contentment can drift with the clouds on a windy day, when the robotic grind starts again, moving from floor to refrigerator to sink to floor. I can sense that something is missing, can't put my finger on it. The malaise doesn't leave, the questioning: Is this all there is? When our children were babies—at one point we had four sons ages three and under—there was no time to ponder the meaning of existence; I was exhausted and hormonal and blissful about surrendering to new motherhood.

A pure state of being apart from the thrashings of the mind was happening big time with our sons, Theo, Isaac, Jack, and Zane. Mothering these boys, our supersonic litter, I was locked into a second-by-second relationship that was full and free, without me having to pour any cerebral energy into it.

I would sit in my kitchen with other mothers, talking, laughing, with no place to go, rocking our babies with our feet in their bouncers on the floor. Yielding to the needs of four small sons was giving me what I had spent a lifetime searching for, a trek that took me through Buddhism and est and Kierkegaard—the ability to experience magic in the moment, peace with what is. Those babies are now strapping boys, ages ten, eight, and six-year-old twins, in school all day, in sports after school. There is more time to think, too much time to think, really.

On some nights that follow ordinary days, unknown characters perform strange scenes in my dreams, dreams that jolt me awake at 3 a.m., sweaty and afraid. The fear is not altogether unpleasant; it serves to remind that this life is not fixed, anything could happen, no matter how beneficent our intentions. Does the desire for change ever cease? How many people can claim to have genuine peace with what is, when it comes to matters of the heart?

I used to turn toward men to make me feel sane and safe; I have found in middle age, as my own mother did, that strong female friendships are what do the trick. I remember Helene Krasnow's sharply shifting moods as a housewife with three young children in the middle 1960s in Oak Park, Illinois. Often when I returned home from school she would be doing crossword puzzles and smoking Kents and sighing so deeply her shoulders would heave. Other afternoons she would be giggly, hugging me harder than usual, singing French love songs while making meat loaf, whipping the red-striped kitchen towel off her shoulder and through the air like a flamenco dancer.

On my mother's happiest days it inevitably turned out she had played Scrabble with her friend Shirley down the street or had clustered with other neighborhood moms to plan a PTA fund-raiser. "The girls," as she called them, never failed to lift her, and although we never talked about it, I realized early on that the closest women in her life were her primary sources for fun and survival. Her circle of women was an escape from housework and the relentless tugs of three kids close in age; they reaffirmed her sense of mission and identity in ways my father, who worked 8:00 a.m. to 6:00 p.m. at an office forty minutes away, could not.

This was before the feminist movement, which birthed all sorts of women's groups. This was before the New Age dawned and both genders began to splinter off into same-sex knots to address hungering souls and hungering hearts and Venus-Mars differences. This was before the unleashing of the Power of the Feminine, catalyzed by books like the 1992 bestseller *Women Who Run with The Wolves* by Clarissa Pinkola Estes and Dr. Christiane Northrup's *Women's Bodies, Women's Wisdom.*

"There is something about the mirroring that you get from other women, where another person says, 'Yes, I hear you,' that fully allows us to accept ourselves and know ourselves," says Washington psychotherapist Marla Zipin. "You can be married to the best husband and the best father, but a man cannot understand what it is like to live in the skin of a woman."

Indeed, the bonds in my own longstanding women's book group cut deep to the marrow, right down to the level where the soul resides. Since we first assembled in Amber Scholtz's dining room in January of 1988, we've collectively been through two marriages, one divorce, four births, one adoption, one cancer surgery, an ongoing battle with diabetes, six deaths of parents, three fiftieth birthdays, and hundreds of bottles of beer and wine. Monthly gatherings with these voracious and raucous women make me feel young and centered and completely loved. I feel as if my life is fully mine to live. This is a group so finely tuned into one another that we notice a three-pound weight loss, the most subtle of hair highlighting, the tiniest trace of depression. We cheer one another's accomplishments, and loathe one another's adversaries.

Leslie remembers that when she suddenly decided to leave her husband of fourteen years, we were 100 percent behind her. Although we were blindsided by her news, we told her we loved her and the choice was obviously right, or else a smart woman like her wouldn't have made it. Leslie says that our meetings served as shelter from the storm, "the only place I could go where I felt totally comforted, totally safe. It was like a nest."

As is usually the case when a couple splits, their friends squared off into opposing camps. Her two grown children were torn in their loyalty to two people they love. The Ladies of the Club liked Leslie's soon to be ex-husband. He was always pleasant and told good jokes. But Leslie is our soul sister, he is not, and whatever Leslie wanted, we wanted, too. We enjoy one another's husbands, have known them all for years, but when there are any complaints from any wife, it is club tradition to rally around our member. It's her team we're on.

This is what every woman I have spoken to tells me she yearns to feel—a sense of wholeness and unconditional love, apart from her identity as a partner to a man. It is the answer to the ancient question that King Arthur searched, unrelentingly, to uncover: "What does Woman really want?" Accord-

ing to legend, King Arthur was ordered to discover this
mystery as a punishment for being caught poaching in the
forests of the neighboring kingdom. An ugly, old, snaggle-
toothed witch agreed to show him the light at this steep price:
King Arthur had to get his closest friend Gawain, the noblest
knight of the round table, to take the witch as his bride. Arthur
persuaded his ever-courteous, chivalrous buddy Gawain to
come through for him. The best interpretation of this tale is
by Jungian storyteller Robert A. Johnson in *Femininity Lost
and Regained*:

"When Gawain was prepared for the wedding bed and
waiting for his bride to join him, she appeared as the loveliest
maiden a man could ever wish to see! Gawain, in his astonish-
ment, asked what had happened," writes Johnson. "The maiden
replied that because Gawain had been courteous to her, she
would show him her hideous side half of the time, and her
gracious side the other half of the time. Which of the two did
he choose for the day and which for the night? . . .

"Noble man that he was, Gawain replied that he would
let the maiden choose for herself. At this, the maiden announced that she would be a fair damsel to him both day and
night, since he had given her respect and sovereignty over her
own life."

So much for critics of feminism who feared that what
woman really wanted was to rule the world. What we wanted
most of all, as King Arthur discovered, is the power to define
and rule ourselves. It is the basic message in the original liber-
ated woman's bible, *Our Bodies, Ourselves: A Book By and For
Women*, first published in 1971, where this proclamation is
made: "In no way do we want to become men. We are women
who are proud of being women. What we do want to do is
reclaim the human qualities culturally labeled 'male' and inte-
grate them with the human qualities that have been seen as
'female' so that we can all be fuller human people."

Barbara Smilow, who teaches a women in the Bible course to Washington-area senior citizens, finds that female fellowships are particularly effective in attempting to unravel some of life's eternal mysteries, such as "Who is God?" Along with teaching the Old Testament, she is also a member of an all-female Bible group she joined in 1984.

At sixty-three, Smilow feels the looming questions brought up in the Bible are increasingly important to her. With three grown children and five grandchildren, she now wants to know, "What's my part in this world?" The women in her group help goad her and guide her, as their most intimate thoughts on God and spirituality come up.

"Women in the group who are feminists don't want a male God, so we spend a lot of time talking about God as a reflection of men," says Smilow. "We talk about what our responsibility to our parents is, and dealing with the loss of a spouse and separating from our children. You can't reinvent these issues every generation, there is a history that comes with them. To look to old literature for answers is soothing."

Smilow began focusing on women as a life-affirming resource in the early 1970s after experiencing what she calls "the explosion of the myth of the fifties"—that is, that it's up to the man to make a woman happy. Her husband Michael was traveling all the time, their three small children were incessantly demanding, she had started reading Simone de Beauvoir's feminist bible *The Second Sex*, and she wanted to flee from her house and life.

"I remember Michael coming home one night, and I was just hostile. And he said, 'What do you want to do? Just tell me. Do you want to want to go somewhere else? Do you want to be someone else?'

"And I was just stunned, because it became clear that it was up to me to decide. And that's when I realized that I can't do this alone, and that this male world isn't going to show me how to do it. So where do you turn? You turn to your women friends."

Indeed, most men I know, including my Chuck, tend to talk around problems. My women friends dive right to the vortex, unabashedly unearthing the truth, making me feel lighter, more hopeful. In part, it can be attributed to basic physiology. Since humans were cave dwellers, females were naturally nurturing and relational, men the aggressors and more evasive. Charles Darwin himself said of the species that it was women who were the more intuitive. Scientists now know that women have better neural connections between the right and left halves of our brains.

"This brain circuitry suggests an explanation for women's intuition," writes Helen Fisher in *Anatomy of Love*. "Perhaps women absorb cues from a wider range of visual, aural, tactile, and olfactory senses simultaneously." With every sensory channel opened at once, no wonder women seem to possess heightened sensitivity and perceptiveness when it comes to re-lationships, sharper radar. We see deep beneath the surface, in all directions.

Husbands often dismiss angst in their wives as hormonal. Between girlfriends, angst is something we don't belittle or try to blame on PMS: we understand that you can have a solid marriage and great children and still experience genuine bursts of sadness, of hungering, of missing something you lost, or perhaps never had. The malaise is not necessarily healthy, but it exists nonetheless and girlfriends don't question it be-cause they recognize their own stirrings about day-to-day dol-drums. Many of us married late, and had too much life under our belts to surrender to marriage without a fight. Thus the malaise, defined in the dictionary as a "vague feeling of dis-comfort or unease," like a stubborn itch in the middle of your back that you cannot reach and that will not go away.

As a newlywed of thirty-three coming off an adventurous

single life, I would sputter my angst over the institution of marriage to my book club sister Leslie, who is a psychotherapist. She always said the same thing: "Iris, lower your expectations." Back then, I told her that I'd never stoop to that, that I'd never surrender to a marriage pocked with bouts of mediocrity and malaise. Yet, Chuck and I—with the help of my wise-women advisors—have survived for twelve years running, with an unshakable love and will to stay married. We've bolstered each other through the deaths of both of our fathers, the near-death of one of our sons, and therapy sessions that felt like Beirut in 1982.

Today, I tell Leslie that she was right. When we expect perfection out of marriage, we are setting ourselves up for disaster. Marriage means tortuous work and a predictable routine; that's what you *should* expect. Indeed, a successful marriage has little to do with sustained bliss, and everything to do with surrendering to the grind. When you ask yourself "is this all there is?" about the spouse you've been sharing a bathroom with for ten or thirty or fifty years, there's a good chance the answer is yes, this *is* it—jackhammer snoring, a man who watches too much sports, a husband who will never change. But if you look hard at what you also have—great kids, a loyal partner, a family unit as an anchor—usually you will discover that all that is yours, however imperfect, is more than enough.

So far, I've spoken from the soul of a woman. Yet, pining for a destiny different than the plot being played out in our own lives is hardly a syndrome exclusive to wives. Richard Ford's collection of romantic fiction, *Women with Men*, introduces a tormented male character who discovers too late that the imperfect life and marriage he fled was actually his sustenance. Martin Austin is married with no children and lives in Oak Grove, Illinois. On a business trip to Paris, he becomes enchanted with Josephine Belliard, a dark-haired Frenchwoman who is estranged from her husband and lives with her young son, Leo. Upon returning to his home outside of Chicago, Austin takes a leave from his job, packs his bags, and abandons his wife, Barbara, "tall and beautiful, confident about her life," to be near Josephine, she of thin lips and strange looks who was cool about their encounter, leaving him not with an invitation to hurry back to Paris but with a blasé, "If you come back, call me."

Martin doesn't call, he simply shows up and rents an apartment, ditching his old life with a wife who had grown painfully familiar, fleeing lovemaking that was "practiced, undramatic . . . like a liturgy which points to but really has little connection with the mysteries and chaos that had once made it a breathless necessity."

Martin reasons, as a man who fears that "ordinary life had the potential to grind you into dust," that he is entitled to seek something more mystical and intangible. After all, you have but one life, and "if something makes you feel good for a moment and no one is crushed by it, what's the use of denying yourself?"

He doesn't contact Josephine for days, then finally telephones her apartment. She tells him she must go out, and he offers to baby-sit her four-year-old boy, Leo. When he arrives at Josephine's apartment, she throws her arms around his neck and kisses him hard. This Frenchwoman, who had him "ridiculously infatuated" in his dreams, is now disappointingly real. "Josephine was dressed in a simple white blouse and a pair of odd, loose-fitting pants that had pictures of circus animals all over them, helter-skelter in loud colors . . . they fit in such a way that her small stomach made a noticeable round bulge below the waistband. Josephine looked slightly fat and a little sloppy."

The disenchantment grows as Josephine goes to her appointment and Martin sits on a bench watching Leo play in the park. He is comparing his women, the one he thought he wanted, and the wife he thought he wanted to leave:

"He could never really love Josephine; that he had to concede. Since in his deepest heart he loved only Barbara, for whatever that was worth," writes Richard Ford of Martin. "Yet, for a moment he felt compelled by Josephine, found her appealing, considered even the possibility of living with her for months or years. Anything was possible.

"But seeing her in her apartment today, looking just as he knew she would . . . had made him feel unexpectedly bleak. And he was savvy enough to know that if he felt bleak now, at the very beginning, he would feel only bleaker later, and that in all likelihood life would either slowly or quickly become a version of hell . . ."

Hell comes quickly when Martin, sunk in his thoughts, loses sight of small Leo, who he is supposed to be watching. After a frantic search, the child is discovered in a clump of yew bushes on a patch of ground that smells of human excrement. Leo has been molested, left naked with his clothes strewn around him, by someone who is never found. Nothing like a hard dose of reality to kill a fantasy romance:

"You are a fool," Josephine tells Martin when she discovers what happened to her son. "I hate you. You don't know anything. You don't know who you are. Who are you? . . . You're nothing." Staying in Paris to search his soul, Martin despairs over the twisted life he has concocted for himself. Josephine, the force that lured him away from his old life, this after a "swelling moment" of promise felt after their first kiss, means nothing now. There was "no fabric or mystery, no secrets, nothing he had curiosity for now." Instead, he knows he will go back to Barbara, yearning to repair what he had broken, to confront his failure as a husband and his tendency to blame his unhappiness on someone other than himself.

"He recognized again and ever more plainly that his entire destination, everything he'd ever done or presumed or thought, had been directed toward Barbara, that everything good was there," writes Ford.

Everything good was there, not in the unknown of Paris, the city of lovers and dreamers, but in the known of Oak Grove, Illinois. There, Martin coached a Little League team sponsored by a friend's linoleum company and lived with a beautiful woman he loved. Josephine has a paunchy belly and will forget him; the slender Barbara has his heart and his history.

THE GRIND OF THE ORDINARY

Romantic highs, the can't-eat-can't-sleep brand, come and go, waning when the new becomes old. Affairs are commonly conducted by two people who have just lost ten pounds and who are on their best behavior and have no shared responsibilities. Being in love in an extramarital affair, a breathlessly, heart-churning state because it involves sneaking around and endless suspense, is one thing. Being in love with a spouse you know better than your sibling and who may wear snore-prevention strips at night is a different story, one that's a challenge to sustain. The master storyteller of tortured love scenarios, William Shakespeare, understood this well. As Germaine Greer writes in *The Female Eunuch*, in the chapter titled "The Middle-Class Myth of Love and Marriage": "There is no romanticism in Shakespeare's view of marriage. He recognized it as a difficult state of life, requiring discipline, sexual energy, mutual respect, and great forbearance; he knew there were no easy answers to marital problems, and that infatuation was no basis for continued cohabitation."

After hearing tale after tale of infatuation, and of the fleeting ecstasy and the prolonged agony that accompanies most affairs, I am thrilled to still be married to the man who is the father of my runny-nosed children because only Chuck would lovingly wipe them. I don't have to starve myself for Chuck; I don't get rid of every stray hair on my body for Chuck, going through the hellish waxing frenzy friends endure before they meet their lovers.

Chuck loved me when I gained fifty-five pounds, pregnant with our twins; he loves the fiber of my being, not the packaging. I am who I really am with Chuck, all shades, from great to horrific, adoring to surly, the whole spectrum that comes with real-time living. When I ask him if he thinks we'll be married forever, he always says: "Sure, why not?" And I always respond: "How do you know that?"

And his answer is always the same: "Because you are my wife."

I'm looking at my honeymoon picture, taken in a villa wedged into a cliff in St. Barts in March of 1988. I'm in a hammock on a balcony surrounded by jagged cliffs, palm fronds fanning me in the tropical breeze. Tunnels of setting sunlight in hues of curry and rose are striping the red tile floor, a floor that was cool and soft under our bare feet in the morning as we scrambled eggs to eat with our croissants; a red tile floor we would lie on under the stars at night, the night wind cooling, licking our sweaty skin. The me on the honeymoon has no gray in her brown hair, no wrinkles on her face; she has never used Zia's Nighttime Renewal cream, something she now applies as routinely as she does toothpaste to her teeth. Her expression is serene, expectant, and most of all, relieved.

After an erratic, exhilarating career as a United Press International reporter interviewing famous people such as Billy Graham, Queen Noor and Yoko Ono, this while carrying on exhilarating romances with a stable of Mr. Wrongs, the honeymoon snapshot reveals a woman who appears ready to surrender to the predictable, the ordinary, to a routine. What I didn't know back then in the St. Bart's paradise, a place where our hearts and bodies were perfectly joined, was that the marriage about to unfold before us, with all its promises of stability, would instead be a stage for havoc.

During our year-and-a-half courtship, Chuck and I would talk often about what we wanted, who we were, what we could become. A Presbyterian minister who lived in Seattle, Bruce Larson, used to tell me that for a marriage to make it, couples need "guts, gonads, and God." The guts piece meant the fortitude to work through problems, gonads meant you stayed hot for each other, and the God piece is obvious, the sharing of spiritual values. On guts and gonads, Chuck and I were doing great. As for God, we had to work that out. I was raised Jewish and Chuck was born Methodist and we came to a place before we got married where we agreed our children would practice Judaism.

We both wanted kids, lots of them, "four before forty" was my husband's prophetic wish expressed on our honeymoon, a wish that came true in 1993 when twin boys, Jack and Zane, were born, joining brothers Theo, three, and Isaac, one. I was thirty-nine, Chuck was thirty-seven, and I can tell you that with four children in diapers, our marriage, even the one with guts, gonads, and God and a blessed swoop of fertile fate, felt like something far different than the forever I was fantasizing about on a cliff, in a hammock, hot with honeymoon fever.

At our wedding in cold Chicago, I wore satin slippers and a red garter underneath a silk shantung dress with no back, trailed by my sister Fran and Chuck's sister Martha, both in blush pink gowns. To the John Lennon song "Imagine," I walked down an aisle lined with red and white roses to my groom, so tall, his hair too long, too curly, just like I liked it, his smile boyish, inviting. I felt relieved to be entering into something traditional with a solid and reliable man, this after too many ephemeral intangibles.

The power of the ordinary would continue to soothe me in the early years of motherhood, a coveted contrast to the splintered years of climbing in my journalism career, searching for meaning and self-identity all over the world. Surrendering to a life of the messy and mundane with four sons all in diapers filled me with sustained passion and wonder and fulfillment. I would sit in my kitchen and watch the amber of sunset on the Severn River while Chuck was upstairs scrubbing four boys in one bathtub, and go over my day: wiping crusted banana off the TV screen, scraping mud off Stride Rite shoes with my Swiss Army Knife, reading *Rapunzel* to four enraptured boys who were looking at their mother with reverence and awe. And I would constantly be reminded that this is as good as it gets. Cranked up on coffee and cornered by kids, finally, I was present in the present of my own life, and not zipping past the now to reach somewhere higher and better.

Passion of the soul, that fire we all seek, was stirred by the mere comfort of fundamental tasks such as waking children, dressing children, feeding children, having them cling to me tightly like monkeys. Motherhood hit me with a blinding epiphany. As someone who spent a lifetime chasing the ultimate feel-good experience in any country I could get to, I was stunned to discover the best sensation of all came from sitting in a rocking chair with one child or four, slumped against my chest. Marriage continues to be a different story. When I wrote *Surrendering to Motherhood*, I was possessed with great clarity. As I write *Surrendering to Marriage*, there are gusts of fog, crashes of heart and mind. I think of the mundane and messy and ordinary forces that shot me with light as a new mother. In marriage, ordinary can be poisonous. In marriage, it's the everydayness that can rip you apart, the deflation that comes from straddling duty and desire.

I am a good mother. I am trying to be a better wife. And

I know that I'm not alone in the struggle because the section from my first book most often cited in correspondence from readers is called "Surrendering to Marriage." It was on these pages that I described a time that Chuck and I came close to ending our marriage. In those newlywed years, when I complained about Chuck being remote and unreachable, our sharp baby-sitter, Bernice, a single mother with three children by two men, used to tell me how lucky I was to be married to him.

"How can you say I'm lucky?" I would demand.

"Because he's home, Iris," Bernice would say. "My men, they were never home."

As recorded in *Surrendering to Motherhood*, here's what our home of tawny shingles designed by my architect husband felt like after a fight in February 1995, when Chuck packed a bag and fled out of the driveway in his red Nissan truck:

> This "four before forty" stuff achieved in less than four years had frayed us to our breaking point. Boggled by four babies and six years of no sleep, we never had the chance to nurture and baby each other. And so there I was, on an idyllic hill flanked by children, looking out my kitchen window at a river, as the man who made my fairy tale come true was adding on an unhappy ending.
>
> There is no way to prepare yourself for the meltdown of a marriage and the liquid pain that swirls through your body, through every space where you walk. It zaps you in the bedroom where his blue terry cloth robe lies like a dead body on the Berber carpet of jewel tones you picked together. It hits you in the bathroom that smells of his Mennen Speed Stick and where his boxers are strewn near the shower. It's a pain that feels like a bullet tearing into your flesh.

*I thought about something Chuck would often say
as I carried on about how we weren't meant to be,
how we weren't meshed in spirit like you must be in
marriage. He'd say in that soft voice that you had to
crane to hear that we were part of a destiny that we
could no longer change, or rearrange. That by making
first one boy, then two, then three, then four, we were
soul mates in the largest sense even if we didn't think
we were, or didn't want to be.*

I am lucky to be his wife, Bernice was right, I'm thinking
this morning in March of 2000 as Chuck is downstairs reading
The Washington Post and eating Multi-Grain Cheerios. Chuck
is home. When he leaves, he comes back, I can count on that.
I can count on him doing what he says he's going to do, unfailingly. He doesn't drink George Dickel whiskey in bars until
dawn with his buddies. Most nights Chuck is on a sweltering
field, swatting bugs, coaching his sons in lacrosse and soccer,
and when winter comes, he switches to basketball. Then, he
hoses the boys down and lies next to them on their beds, coaxing them to sleep with whispered promises of what's going to
happen the next day. We still get in bad tiffs, but over time we
have learned not to run from each other, we stay in the cage;
we are a family, we have to, where would we go?

I love Chuck. He can fix toilets and leaky roofs, he builds
Adirondack chairs with driftwood, he wears a tool belt. I'm a
sucker for a guy who can do chores, I mean *real* chores. Could
it really be better the second time around, parenting old children with an ex, while you live with someone new, a man
who doesn't own a chain saw? Many people who have ended
marriages and moved on to new partners describe a love that
can never achieve its full bloom, a muffled happiness because
of kids who aren't in their constant custodial care. Yet, one
can't help but feel a pang when a middle-aged friend makes a

fresh start, how she tremors with youthfulness. In the words of nineteenth-century philosopher Søren Kierkegaard, "What wine is so sparkling, so fragrant, so intoxicating, as possibility?"

There have been many junctures where we were ready to bail. It seems to happen every December actually, when we are swirling through the holiday madness and thrust into our own childhood memories of Hanukkah and Christmas and being safe and loved by our own mothers and fathers. It's a time each of us wants to be taken care of, not taking care of others. One of our worst December brawls took place during a car ride in Washington, D.C., on our way to a dinner party. Chuck said something nasty about the people giving the party, *my* friends not his, I said something meaner, he said something unforgivable, and I flung a wrapped box holding an antique blue-and-white bowl at Chuck, a gift we were bringing to the hosts. We heard the shatter and opened the box to find that the eggshell-thin Chinese porcelain bowl had broken in three pieces. We quickly stopped to pick up a bottle of wine as a replacement gift and didn't speak the whole night—thankfully, it was one of those dinner parties where husbands and wives are placed on opposite ends of a table.

The next morning I sat in the kitchen drinking coffee and staring at the broken bowl. I couldn't throw it out; it was wonderful and it wasn't cheap and Chuck and I had picked it out together over a lunch hour at one of our favorite shops in Dupont Circle. So I got out some Superglue and painstakingly put the pieces back together, taking lots of time to precisely line up the edges and make sure the glue didn't glob. Chuck came down to breakfast and stared at the bowl, which looked nearly good as new. He didn't say anything, but he looked at it silently for just long enough for me to understand that he understood that making that bowl we loved whole again was a symbol of something larger. We still have that bowl, and

we've never said a word about it, but I know we both appreciate the fact that I repaired it and didn't throw the pieces away.

The Superglue made the fragile object stronger than it
was before it broke, and it never fails to remind me of our
marriage, which has felt broken time and time again, but we
always fix it, not with permanent cement, but with an uncanny
will to put the pieces back together. And each time our relationship severs and we succeed at repairing it, the marriage
emerges in a form that is a little more unbreakable. Yes, this
marriage is starting to feel like a rock that is so embedded in
the earth that it can't be budged, so solid it can't be smashed.
It feels like a force that no fight, no matter how nasty and
hurtful, can eviscerate. The long-marrieds I spoke with agree
that partnerships over time become sturdier, the points and
jagged surfaces become smooth and soft, and the sheer weight
of a shared life is so heavy you have no other choice but to
surrender, because the mass cannot be overturned.

I was staring at the blue-and-white, patched-together
bowl yesterday in the living room while talking on the porta-
ble phone. A married friend in Texas was calling, hysterical, to
tell me she had finally ended her on-again, off-again affair.
Beatrice called me often. When I was feeling sad about marriage and she was ebullient about her lover, I would wonder if
I was missing some boat myself that would take me to a more
exotic and beautiful land. But as her bouts of depression
started to outnumber her bouts of joy, her stories evoked not
envy, but pity. Nothing is more effective at nipping my own
cravings for a fling, or helping to heal ambiguity about the
grind of marriage, than her desperate phone calls or twisted
stories from other friends in affairs.

I've seen plump and normal women turn skeletal and
manic because of obsessions with men who are married, or
are simply unavailable. I've seen serial-adulterer husbands in
comfortable marriages become numb with shock when the

"unsexy" wives they took for granted suddenly announced they wanted out because they had fallen hard for someone else. No one can tell you that affairs are ultimately fulfilling; most people will tell you they are ultimately debilitating. And over time, fantasy lovers go poof and flawed humans are revealed, with disgusting habits and stupid sides to their personalities.

Yet, even though we know that commitment is more gratifying than hot, forbidden sex, this grounded, moral wisdom that comes from maturity is still not enough to snuff out all desire to be naughty once in a while, a desire piqued by poetry such as this unforgettable line from the ancient, poem Song of Solomon: "Thou hast ravished my heart." Every heart needs a bit of ravishing, to be awoken from the languor. The malaise may hide, but it never vanishes altogether.

The malaise erupts like lava from a dormant burble when we are reminded of what perfect love feels like by a panting friend who is convinced she has found the real thing for the first time, ever. I'm thinking of Beatrice in Texas, in a long affair with a married man. She used to tell me that she'd stand lathering herself slowly in the steamy shower, bursting with a happiness "that shoots like a fountain," as she imagined him. Her description reminds me of a Marc Chagall painting, his floaty women, ripe, expectant, and nude. We feel the longing when we stumble upon a molten passage in a great book, such as this one by James Joyce in *Ulysses*: ". . . and then I asked him with my eyes to ask again yes and then he asked me would I yes . . . and first I put my arms around him yes and drew him down to me so he could feel my breasts all perfume yes and his heart was going like mad and yes I said yes I will Yes."

Yes, I will, yes, Yes. But I can't. Because the twins are getting their teeth cleaned at 4 p.m., and the two older boys have lacrosse practice at six, and I need to get home between that time to make dinner for my husband—so not tonight.

Who among us is not conflicted, some more deeply than others, about what it means to love a spouse? The only permanent quality you can expect in marriage is that your response to the partnership will always be changing. You can expect the sting of Cupid's arrow to fade, the ahas to turn into ho-hums at times. And you can expect, when you least expect it, to feel rapturous on a rainy morning when the kids are at religious school and it's just the two of you sprawled across a king-size bed. When rapture is replaced by the dread routine, we remember and we mourn what Ethel Person captures in *Dreams of Love and Fateful Encounters*: "Love arises from within ourselves as an imaginative act, a creative synthesis, that aims to fulfill our deepest longings and our oldest dreams, that allows us both to renew and transform ourselves."

It's all so selfish, really, being in love. The more deeply we love another depends on how deeply he or she makes us love ourselves.

IS THIS ALL THERE IS?

On a leaden morning between Christmas and New Year's Day, my forty-year-old friend Chloe was at Starbucks lamenting over marriage. Playing with the charms on her necklace, a boy inset with a sapphire and a girl in a garnet skirt, she winced at the memory of a train ride a decade ago when she was first dating the man who would become her spouse. They kissed and laughed like teenagers from Washington, D.C., to New York City. Today she is the mother of his children, two toddlers she loves deeply. But her husband, she says, sometimes makes her feel "sad and confused." Her complaints revolve around these recurring themes.

"We do not connect."

"If it weren't for the kids, this marriage would be over."

"I miss feeling passion."

In many ways, hers is a classic voice on modern, big-city, two-career relationships. I've heard it over and over. Chloe is a partner in an advertising firm, and many of her clients are based in Europe and the Middle East. She has thus far been loyal to her husband of fourteen years, but with alluring travel and stimulating new friendships from the workplace, she's finding it harder to stay focused on the tight limits of family life. Here is more from Chloe:

Traditionally, a wife is supposed to be in a nurturing role. She nurtures the children, she nurtures the husband, and her focus should be directed inward, to them. But my position is that my husband and I live side by side, and because of the demands of my career, much of the time I am focused outward. He wanted me to focus into him; that's why he is so lonely.

My mother was not a doting mother and therefore I was not raised to be a doting wife. I wasn't brought up to believe that I'm here to take care of my man. And here's my husband who is counting on me to provide a homey feeling for him, support and sexiness, but I'm so wrapped up in my work and the stress of that, plus coping with small children, I don't have time to take care of his enormous needs.

When the kids were born, I went through this maternal phase where I didn't crave sex at all. Snuggling with the children was enough. Now I'm feeling much warmer toward my husband, but it's still a constant struggle just to make sure I'm pleasant toward him because my head is usually going in a hundred other directions.

The empowerment of women on all levels has been so intimidating for men. I think men are emasculated. Men don't have this almighty position they used to have. I mean, they were in total control, we were possessions. Now we're not possessions, we're companions. We both get home at 7 p.m., and both look into an empty refrigerator. I can't snap my fingers and create a hot meal. And I can't snap my fingers and be this doting wife. I just don't have the energy after a long, stressful day of work, and after two hours of being with the kids before bedtime, to go sit down by candlelight and look in my husband's eyes and listen to his problems. At that point of my day, I just want to tune out the world and tune into myself.

Lately, since I've lost my pregnancy weight, I'm feeling a lot better about myself, more attractive. That has rekindled my sexual desire for my husband. Even though marriage can feel pretty blah, I'm entering a midlife high about who I am. And although I do hope I can make this marriage last forever—we do have these children—I can't say for sure we will. I feel like the world's infinite and we can find many people who are qualified for us. I am married to someone who is very needy emotionally, and who just may need to move on to someone who can give him more than I do in that area.

It's interesting, I notice that the better I feel about myself the more irritated my husband seems to get. A lot of the male self-esteem comes from a woman who will just stare into their eyes and hang onto every word and be totally enraptured with what they have to say and that's not who I am. I can't rustle up that kind of energy and enthusiasm anymore. Frankly, I'm too busy and tired for that.

Having said that, I'll tell you what I miss. I miss romance. I feel like I need a total escape. I need the thrill of a new face. I need a new flirtation. I need to be around someone who makes me feel like a vital force. And I'm not getting that from my husband. I know flirtations can be dangerous, especially for someone like me because I'm the type of person who would fall deeply, madly in love. I do love my husband, but of course, that's a different love, isn't it?

Marriage is an unnatural state. It's just very hard to remain romantic with someone you live with. Everyone we know is seeing *a therapist, and most of those people aren't getting to a better place in their marriages. The problem is, if you think your spouse has difficult traits, those traits only get worse with age. And who wants to put up with that?*

One week later I got a call from a childhood friend who now lives in Colorado. Liza was elated with the news that she was divorcing her doctor husband of eighteen years for the "love of my life," a champion runner she met at work. My friend told me that her daughter, an only child and a senior in high school, was a "mess," but getting better. The shrieks of my own four small sons in our Annapolis kitchen drowned her out at several points, but this part I didn't miss. This swatch of the phone call from my old pal, reborn at forty-three, I heard clearly, and will never forget:

"Although I always felt totally secure financially and emotionally, I've had a deep hunger for years," she started out softly. "Anytime I made an overture to talk about something intellectual, or to do something fun with my husband, he would say, 'I don't feel like it.' But I never thought of leaving him, I believed 'this is as good as it gets.' I thought, 'Okay, I'll go to the theater with someone else. Okay, I'll take vacations with someone else. I thought I was just fine. Then I met the most incredible man at work."

Liza began to giggle, sounding like the girl she was all those summers with me at overnight camp. Her voice became husky and reverent. "I felt like I found my soul mate; it was like I had been deprived, and then suddenly I woke up in every way. Here was a man who was passionate about life and about me. My husband and I had sex once every couple of weeks. It wasn't great sex, it was normal sex, the same kind of sex we had always had." More giggles. "But it was sex that I now know to be really substandard."

I hung up the phone and stuck a jumbo Stouffers macaroni and cheese dinner into the oven. Wearing a dish towel over one shoulder of a baggy velour sweatsuit, I pictured Liza in short shorts, hiking in the Rocky Mountains with her great-sex, soul mate. I thought about all the people close to me, males and females, trying so hard to make their marriages endure, for the children, out of fear of failure, out of a fear of starting over, out of a sense of moral duty. Surveying the whole group, I could come up with only a few couples who were having a relatively easy time, and almost no one who wasn't in marriage therapy—or didn't want to be.

Judging from the spate of relationship literature in the vein of *Fighting for Your Marriage* by Howard Markman, I know my little group is not an isolated example. Pick up any lifestyle magazine any month and you are continually hit by articles like "Twenty-five Ways to Make Your Marriage Hot Again." Despite the shift from random love to a revival in family values and monogamy, marital angst is as central to the times as recycling and heart-healthy cuisine. This angst is our generational cliché.

There are now more than 50,000 licensed marriage and family therapists in the United States, a fifty-fold increase since 1970, according to figures from the American Association for Marriage and Family Therapy. And while there is a strengthening marriage-preservation movement in our country among therapists, the clergy, and even some lawyers, half of marriages still end in divorce. Barbara Dafoe Whitehead calls America "a society of the uncommitted" in her book *The Divorce Culture.*

This turbulence that aging baby boomers are experiencing from trying to sustain permanent unions comes as no surprise. The unleashed hippies turned yuppies who had it all in the eighties can't be expected to settle into predictable, placid roles. Staying still with one person in one place clashes with the psyche of a generation reared on spiritual exploration and individual growth. We yearn to remain riding the Yellow Submarine rather than flopped on a couch splattered with purple Juicy Juice, next to a spouse clicking through TV channels.

I told Washington clinical psychologist Dr. Isaiah Zimmerman, a couples specialist who has been in practice for nearly fifty years, that the same theme keeps playing over and over with too many of my married friends: That although they are trying madly to keep their marriages and families intact, they miss feeling madly in love.

Zimmerman blames much of their despair on what he calls the "have-it-all syndrome." This is a phenomenon he is seeing increasingly in his office among middle-aged couples—a compulsion to have everything and feel cheated if they come up short of that goal.

"It's what I call totalistic thinking, that you are somehow entitled to have it all," Zimmerman explains. "This comes out of a powerful social expectancy today that you can have it all—as in being socially secure, sexually secure, financially secure, and having high-achieving children. Disappointment is inevitable, because nobody can have it all, as an individual or as a couple.

"It helps to be a little more realistic, to accept limitations," he continues. "Intimacy and love take very continuous, very hard work. But working things through over time is not ingrained in this culture: You are used to immediacy. I am seeing a surprising return to trying to make marriages survive, but nonetheless while you are committed to your partners, you are still not happy. Because you are not fulfilling the dream you carried from the sixties, a dream of unlimited possibilities in life."

This inability to let go of a need for peak experiences isn't made any simpler by the dictum of the New Age: Seek relationships that go soul to soul. The term *soul mate* often doesn't describe that person who shouts car pool schedules and shoves overdue bills at you over the cacophony of your screaming kids. Fearing that one's true soul mate is out there waiting and a more soulful life could be had leaves many people hankering for something or someone else. And it's not just the men hankering, like it used to be. With women now pervasive in all professions, there is equal opportunity to meet a parade of potential mates. In our parents' generation, women stayed home and their primary prospects for some romance on the side were the milkman or the gas man.

Our parents in their rigid and restricted roles had a different take on the meaning of "I do." Rocked by the Depression and innocent about relationships, they generally surrendered to marriage without a backward glance. They didn't dwell on whether they were happily married. They were married, period, for better and for worse.

"It never once occurred to me to leave my marriage," says Roz Morrow, a Maryland mother of four and grandmother of eight who married her husband Stan at the age of nineteen. In their forty-six years together, she has bolstered her husband through two heart surgeries, the removal of one of his kidneys, and prostate cancer. He helped her through her recent spine surgery and learning to walk again.

"I come from a time when you went straight from your parents' home to your marriage home, so it wasn't like I ever missed this old, glamorous life," she adds. The jaded offspring of those with Morrow's 1950s sensibility harbor too many adrenaline-laced memories to go down without a fight.

We feel as if sustained happiness is a right that we are owed, a promise from vintage rock 'n' roll that we're going to be taken higher and higher. That everything is going to be all right. But it's not all right, it hurts and it's hard. Love is supposed to be passionate, not practical. We don't want to give up feeling like a character in a D. H. Lawrence novel:

"She dared to let go everything, all herself, and be gone

in a flood. Now all her body clung with tender love to the unknown man. . . . It had been so perfect . . . ," Lawrence writes in *Lady Chatterley's Lover*. Sublime romance, borne of the dreams of poets and novelists, is a dangerous tease that amplifies the abysses in our own earthly and ordinary relationships. We become intoxicated by the lonely housewife portrayed by Meryl Streep and the roving photographer played by Clint Eastwood alone in the kitchen of a desolate farmhouse in the film *Bridges of Madison County*. We never follow the players into scenes of boredom and estrangement and battling.

In the dawn of the millennium, the hippest of love doctors are telling us that getting real about marriage and divorcing it from romantic love is necessary for a union that lasts. This New Marriage is one forged out of surrender, to tortuous daily work, to realizing that being happily married doesn't necessarily guarantee that you get to be happy. Surrender means understanding to the bone the meaning of commitment, as "a promise, a pledge." So we go to shrinks to fix our dysfunctional selves made so by our own dysfunctional families, all the while grumbling that being in love should be easier, that if we were truly right for each other we wouldn't have to try so damned hard to make it work. Making a marriage last can seem like the impossible dream, as if Simone de Beauvoir, who likened matrimony to slavery, was right when she wrote: "Individuals are not to be blamed for the failure of marriage: it is . . . the institution itself, perverted as it has been from the start."

Here's what the institution of marriage has come to after a century redefined by feminism, the sexual revolution, the divorce revolution, and self-obsession: Couples can now discover whether they are indeed happy, or hopeless, by signing up to be examined at the Family Research Laboratory on the Seattle campus of the University of Washington. Led by the divorced and remarried psychologist John Gottman, author of

The Seven Principles for Making Marriage Work, the laboratory is equipped with video cameras and pulse and sweat monitors that supposedly translate hidden emotions as spouses respond to questions designed to crack open areas of conflict, such as sexual satisfaction and sharing of responsibilities. Throughout their conversation in the love lab, heart rates and other twitches and twitters are interpreted as defensiveness, contempt, and belligerence, traits Gottman considers guaranteed precursors to divorce. By using machines to measure compatibility, long believed to be an inexplicable meshing of human spirits, Gottman claims he can predict with 90 percent accuracy whether or not a couple has what it takes for an enduring marriage.

I'd rather listen to the stirrings in my heart than to signals from electrodes. The new, cold science of love tends to dissipate the magic we were taught could be ours, the brand Bob Dylan sings to his Sara when he calls her his sweet virgin angel, the sweet love of his life, radiant jewel, mystical wife. As much as we'd like to soar on the wings of poets like Dylan who avert our attention away from the tedious mechanics of marriage to its mystery, it appears that grit and perseverance get you the love of your life more than mysticism. Dylan himself knew this to be true: After his 1977 divorce from Sara, the mother of his four children, he had this to say about marriage: "People fall in love with a person's body . . . with the way they dress, with their scorecards. With everything but their real selves, which is what you need to love if you're to be happy together."

Here's what lies ahead should you choose to keep working on loving the one you are with: A survey published in the fall of 1997 in the *Social Psychology Quarterly* reported that couples who make it to their thirty-fifth anniversary find themselves as happy with each other as they were when they were newlyweds, this after happiness steadily declines for the first twenty years of marriage. As sociologist Terri Orbuch noted in the study: "Declines in work and parental responsibilities explain a large portion of the increase in marital satisfaction in later years. . . ."

Certainly we should be satisfied with core qualities like stability and friendship in a marriage. Certainly we should be smart enough to realize that steady is better than intense when it comes to love in the long haul. But here lies the rub for a population seduced by soul: Can *satisfied* ever *really* be enough for those who spun out of an illusory era of cosmic dreams? After fifty-five years of marriage, Washington interior decorator Gloria Liebenson says it should be.

She was only twenty-one when she stood with Herbert Liebenson before a justice of the peace in North Carolina. Yet, even at that young age, she remembers feeling certain about her decision to be married, not ambivalent like many older newlyweds of today.

"I think people were a lot happier back then, even with the Depression, I really do, because life was less complicated," Liebenson starts out. "We weren't exposed to all this crap out there today, and we didn't have fifty different career paths open to us. The man worked and the woman usually stayed home, and one income per family was enough.

"I also married in an era when divorce was not an option," she continues. "In those days, you couldn't say *cancer* out loud, you said *the big C*. Divorce was the same thing, you said *the big D*, you would never discuss it. It was a disgrace in the family. We never said, 'Well, if it doesn't work out we could always end it.' People got married and that was that."

Robert Liotta, one of Washington's most sought-after divorce lawyers, hears story after story detailing the frayed intimacy that results from unmet bottom-line expectations. He says that one of the "classic cases" in his twenty-five years of practice is a husband or wife initiating divorce because the kids have grown and in the absence of child-rearing chores, the barren state of the marriage becomes glaringly clear.

"I can't tell you the number of people in their forties and fifties who come in my office and haven't had a sexual relationship with their spouses for eight, ten, even fifteen years—it shocks me," says Liotta. "These are the couples who stay together until the kids go off to college, then someone says to the other person, 'Hey, we don't have much of a relationship left, I'm outta here.'"

Chuck and I had been married two-and-a-half years when a special issue of *Time* magazine titled "Women: The Road Ahead" arrived in the mail highlighting the postfeminism struggles of blending careers, marriage, and family. It was fall of 1990, we had a ten-month-old son, and I was experiencing my own psychic meltdown over having left the sexy and ego-pumping field of daily journalism to be a mother at home. With a new baby and no full-time career for the first time in fifteen years, my read on marriage was that it was the heaviest load I had ever taken on. It had been difficult enough living with myself for all these years; now a stranger, this one my opposite—hard and withdrawn to my soft and open—was incessantly in my face, in the bathroom mirror brushing his teeth when I needed it to apply mascara, watching ESPN when I wanted CNN, sleeping when I was awake, awake when I was asleep.

Since my freshman year in college, I had been a devotee of the *I Ching*, seeking the Taoist balance of yin and yang, or melding of masculine and feminine energies.

"If we hold the Tao within, joy will surely follow," promises passage thirty-five from the *I Ching*. This ancient belief that opposing traits somehow create a unified and balanced energy field was a motivator in my own spouse selection. Chuck Anthony was carved of classic yang—rational, left-brainy, stoic. And I was a textbook yin—yielding, right-brainy, emotional. He grew up in a farming town near the Chesapeake Bay, Centreville, Maryland, population 2,000. I am from Chicago. His maternal and paternal descendants settled in Maryland in the early 1700s. My father's parents were from Russia, settling in the United States in the early 1900s. My mother is from Warsaw, Poland, and after spending the World War II years in Paris, she moved to Chicago in 1950. To the Anthony family, the Krasnow family is like a *National Geographic* special, and vice versa. It doesn't get much more yin and yang.

After a year of marriage, pregnant with our first child, the yin-yang equation started to feel like a star-crossed disaster, not harmonious and spiritually right, but combustible and wrong. Our psyches were at war, not united like the two paisley-shaped lobes of the yin-yang emblem that meld into one circle.

Some sense of solidarity came from reading a survey in that 1990 issue of *Time* on the future of women, in which unmarried college students, keen observers of their own baby boom aunts, uncles, and parents, were asked: "How difficult is it to have a good marriage today?" Three-quarters of the respondents, male and female, put their mark in the categories "very difficult" or "difficult." That was the painful prediction a decade ago; today, marriage is even more difficult, a word described in the dictionary as "hard to understand or deal with," as all of our lives have accelerated along with rapid technology, leaving few blanks in our calendar for romance and playtime.

At the start of a new century, email and cell phones and beepers and faxes have a monopoly over our attention and time, ripping into the therapeutic moments couples require to connect with each other one on one, eye to eye. Grinding through the hours as multitaskers trying to do everything at once, who has the mind-set to relax at day's end and communicate? It's easier to seal off with a couple of martinis either at home or with a coworker you have a crush on, someone who worships you, doesn't criticize you, offers everything you feel like you don't get from your spouse.

Here's the cold truth: Overscheduled and overwhelmed, splayed between kids and career, most folks find it extraordinarily tough to create a smooth marriage day to day. The truth is that bliss may be there at dawn and gone by lunch, and that there are as many times that you feel like saying "Screw you" as you feel like saying "I love you."

One morning after a bad spat with Chuck, I was weighing our odds at marital survival. We had been bickering over something stupid—I insisted that many low-fat foods were high in carbohydrates and he said I was wrong, although it turned out I was right—and the disagreement escalated into a drizzle of cold coffee tossed from my mug missing his clean, white starched shirt by a hair, but spraying the bedroom wall. I took off in my blue Suburban, turned on the radio only to hear Simon and Garfunkel singing "Hello darkness my old friend, I've come to talk with you again."

I cried and cried over the darkness in my heart, a heart that was a cave of hope and light when I was a woman just engaged, drinking Schramsberg champagne with her prince in an A-frame cabin in Berkeley Springs, West Virginia. Darkness does become a familiar, old friend when you're working at a marriage for years and you keep getting tripped up by sniping over who's right, who's wrong, who neglected to do what chore.

Yet, I carry on and most of my friends carry on, weathering frustration and loneliness and disappointment, and surrendering to imperfect relationships. Some cannot fathom the ordinariness of marriage, the everydayness, the lukewarm, and instead of stoking dying home fires, they choose to go get hot elsewhere.

I have two close girlfriends with young children who recently broke up long-term, lukewarm marriages to be with people they love madly. As one of them put it: "I traded in a doughy, boring husband for an exciting, rock-hard man. I have never had better sex in my life. With my husband, I had to do all sorts of mental gymnastics during our sex in order to have an orgasm. With this man, I get fully aroused just looking at him standing naked in front of me." My other friend's children are not sleeping well, waking up shrieking from nightmares. But when this forty-one-year-old woman looks at me with the eyes of a teenager off to the prom, and relays how she does stripteases for her beau during their lunch hour, how she's never been skinnier, has never felt sexier, I'm not sure how to respond when she says: "In time, the children will be fine. Don't I deserve to be happy?"

On the one hand, I want to tell my friend-in-lust that infatuation inevitably withers, that all it will take is a month of sharing a bathroom for the ecstasy to subside. On the other hand, I want her life.

Last summer, I was driving our children home from school when still another marital casualty was reported over my cell phone lines. A prominent journalist had just received news that his wife, the mother of his two small children, was in love with a woman in her twenties. A girlfriend has chosen to stay in her long-term, mediocre, sexless marriage but indulges in screwathons behind tinted windows in her minivan up to three times a week with one of her husband's friends, a man she loves madly. Their interludes have taken place for the past two years in the parking lot of a medical center.

I know a married bed-and-breakfast owner who is sleeping with one of her waiters, a boy just out of college who so titillates her with his touch and attention that she is thinking of leaving her eight-year-old daughter with her husband for a while and running away with Junior Stud out West somewhere. Stella got her groove back, says this thirty-six-year-old woman, and she's not about to let it go—this after thirteen years of below-average sex with a husband known for philandering.

As early as 1953 in the extensive study conducted by Alfred Kinsey and documented in the book *Sexual Behavior in the Human Male,* more than a quarter of the married women who were interviewed admitted to at least one act of adultery; the corresponding percentages for American males was 50 percent. This is the book in which Kinsey declared that a man would be promiscuous "throughout the whole of his life if there were no social restrictions."

Nearly fifty years later, in a society with very lax social restrictions, we all know of marital cheating going on—or about to go on. Despite the rampant buzz, infidelity remains a tough trend to track with accurate statistics or credible studies. For one thing, few people tell the truth about their sexual escapades. A decade ago, Peggy Vaughan, who coauthored the book *Beyond Affairs* with her husband James Vaughan and whose full story you will hear later, estimated that 60 percent of men and 40 percent of women will have extramarital affairs. With the advent of Internet romances and increasing numbers of women in the workforce, Vaughan says today that figure is nearing 60 percent for females, too.

Statistics vary among researchers gauging sexual behavior among marrieds, but this fact no one can dispute—once in the closet, affairs have been outed. Relationship sections of any large bookstore carry a growing selection of survival guides for victims of cheating hearts, penned by love mavens and scorned spouses. Entire therapy practices are now built around counseling couples coping with the pain and betrayal of adultery. Yet, the experience is still indelible. Frieda is a septuagenarian in New York City whose husband of fifty years strayed some twenty years ago with his secretary. She says forget all this junk about forgiving and forgetting: "You never get over it. I am still angry at him. I still think, How could he? I still cry. You live with it, but it does not leave you, it does not leave your marriage."

However deep is the damage it wreaks, adulterous impulses and forbidden romance is as intrinsic to human behavior as eating, and has been since the time when King David seduced Bathsheba, the wife of Uriah, one of his soldiers. The sweet suffering of unrequited love is epitomized in the fifth-century tale of Phaedra's love for Hippolytus, the stepson of her husband Theseus, the King of Athens. Possessed with a passion that could not be consummated, Phaedra killed herself. As far back as 18 B.C., when Augustus was attempting to tame the phallus-worshipping wildness of Rome's upper class by imposing strict marriage laws, the randy writer Ovid was documenting the adulterous underbelly that existed in his day in *The Art of Love*, a how-to manual on seduction:

"If you are ever caught, no matter how well you've concealed it, though it as clear as the day, swear up and down it's a lie," Ovid advised.

Fudging the truth about one's whereabouts also comes to mind in a centuries-old Indian tale involving Lord Krishna, apparently an Adonis to the women. According to legend, the provocative and lyrical notes of Krishna's flute enticed young wives to tear soundlessly from their husbands' sides to dance by moonlight next to their gorgeous young god.

Mad hunger for someone unattainable is also played out time and time again in modern literature. We can't get enough of it, it's the plot that makes for the sort of book you can't put down. In her bestseller *The Saving Graces*, which depicts the abiding friendships in a women's group set in Washington, D.C., author Patricia Gaffney has the character of Emma pining for the much-married artist Mick. Although Gaffney's book was published in 1999, the emotions she describes are timeless:

"It's true that I hurt all over because of the hopelessness

of this infatuation, but at the same time I'd never felt so alive," laments Emma. "It was the fact that Mick and his legs and his long back and his hard stomach were forbidden to me that made them so unbearably attractive . . ."

Adultery, however devastating it is for the participants, will never die out because human animals will instinctively continue to do what they need to do in order to feel alive. And that means sampling the forbidden, tasting the new. In Stendahl's book *Love,* we read of the basic conflict that arises in long-term relationships: "A man in love sees every perfection in the object of his love, but his attention is still liable to wander after a time because one gets tired of anything uniform, even perfect happiness. . . . The stronger your character, the slighter the impulse to inconstancy."

Partnership without Passion

Yet, we all know people of character, charitable and upstanding, who can't say no to the temptation of new love. Wanderlust is more apt to occur as an escape response to a cold marriage. When the relationship feels barren, adult humans think like animals, with their gonads.

Cindy is a forty-year-old military wife from South Carolina with three young children, a kitchen where a terra-cotta angel hangs over shelves of food-stained cookbooks, a job as a nurse, and not a brown hair out of place. Her front door has a wreath of dried roses on the door. She goes to Presbyterian church every Sunday morning with her husband, a retired commander, in a crewneck sweater and a crisp, navy skirt that falls right at the knee. Beneath the L.L. Bean veneer, away from her oven, where her famous biscotti is usually baking, a longterm affair and a husband who doesn't want sex have silently been ripping her apart. Here is her story:

When I met my husband, I was twenty-four, and on the rebound from another relationship. I never got hit with a ton of bricks. He was always patient, steady, he was everybody's friend. I mean, he was a great guy. And he fell just madly in love with me, and it felt good, but I still wasn't feeling that passion. I loved his personality; it was definitely not the sex that I loved. Frankly, we just never had sex. And it bothered the hell out of me.

When we did get married, I had never even slept with him, and you know, we've been married fifteen years, and it's still very few and far between, like once a year. We went to counseling once, and he sat there, all clammed up, refused to discuss it. I still think he's a great guy. But we have just about no physical intimacy. He's like a brother, a friend, there's just no touching. I wrote him a letter once telling him that I felt like he wasn't attracted to me, and that he pays more attention to our three children than he does to me. And he didn't respond at all.

He's just a very bottled-in male, just like his father. He will not talk about his feelings; he talks about sports. My husband was away a lot on military assignments, and there was this couple who lived in the same neighborhood with us. And the husband and I seemed to keep the same hours, so we would talk in the morning. It became obvious that we were very drawn to each other. It started up, really, quite easily.

We have a lot in common. We're both Protestant. We both like to cuddle. And his marriage was not the greatest either. One night he had tickets to go to a play and he said, "You want to go? Get a baby-sitter." After the play, we had a few drinks downtown, then in the middle of the street he just stopped, turned around, gave me a huge kiss, and said, "I love you." And that night, he came back to my house, and it kind of just went on from then. It was his second affair in his marriage, but he told me, "You are the real one, and there will never be anyone else."

He was just a very sexual man, and ours was a very passionate relationship. We would have sex all the time, four and five times a week, not just in our houses, in cars, in parking lots, wherever we could. This went on for more than two years. You know, I felt justified. I wasn't getting any sex from my husband. My boyfriend, or whatever you want to call him, kept sleeping with his wife, and that really bothered me. Then a few months ago, they moved to another city.

You know what I miss? I miss him coming over, when we would sit on the couch and talk and he would rub my feet. I miss having someone to hug. I miss knowing that someone thinks I'm pretty. This whole thing just makes me so sad. Here I found what felt like my soul mate, a man I feel passionate about, and instead I'm stuck with my same old life. I went to counseling recently, alone, to our church minister, and I was just bawling. I said, "I just love this man to death." And the minister advised me to cut off all contact, then truly work on my marriage, and if after a year, my love for the other man was still blazing, then maybe it was the right thing to explore that relationship.

But I couldn't let go. Because it's just so lonely with my husband. He comes home from work and I talk to him about what I did today, and he's totally tuned into the television. And then right in the middle of my story, he'll dive on the floor and give our dog a big hug, and start wrestling him. And I'm thinking, How about a hug and a wrestle for me?

I went to see the minister again and told him that my husband and I have gone nine months without sex, he was amazed. His jaw dropped. Yet, I still see myself staying married, and it will just never be a romantic relationship. So this is my life. I'm married to a man who is a great father to children he loves. He does his share of the housework. He goes to work everyday. He doesn't drink to excess. He doesn't beat me. We have enough money. We have a lot of friends. He is active in the community, and everybody who knows him adores him.

There is one big problem: There is no intimacy whatsoever. So we do other things. We play golf. We play tennis. For a while,

I would come to bed in a sexy nightgown, but that didn't seem to work. And you know, I'm not ugly. I'm not fat. Every once in a blue moon, when we do have sex, I say, "Let's do this more often, because it is fun and I think it would make us closer." But he just laughs. The children are my only source for bodily contact. I don't know what I'll do when they are gone.

Something horrible happened recently with me and my boyfriend, and it made me see who he really is. He called me last week, and he was totally disgusting on the telephone. Oh my God, I just couldn't believe it. He told me that "the shit has hit the fan." I found out that he has been involved with still another woman and his wife found out. He met this new woman, girl really, she's in her twenties, because they both run marathons. Apparently she is married, too, and get this, she has a six-month-old baby. I mean, how screwed up can this be?

Then he tells me, "I want to spend the rest of my life with this woman," same thing he used to tell me. He even had the gall to tell me, "Boy, does she have an unbelievable body." Oh my God, if I could see him now, I would just spit in his face. He is a complete ass, and he is also a complete coward, because he'll just keep having affairs, and he will never divorce his wife.

I don't hate myself for what I've done, because it has made me realize that what I do have may not be the most perfect thing in the world, but my husband does love me. He's an honest man. I talked to the minister about whether or not I should tell my husband everything, and he asked me, "Who would this make feel better, you or him? You may feel like you need to get this off your chest but telling your husband would just tear him apart."

So here's my big challenge. How am I going to live out the rest of my marriage without physical intimacy? And I don't know the answer to that. I have not discounted the possibility that I may meet someone else.

After a long night listening to Cindy's tape, I thought about how surprised many husbands would be if they knew about the number of wives on the prowl, uptight women they would never expect to wander. Something ferocious seems to transpire in the belle epoque of females in their forties; exploding hormones have the potential to run ramshackle over reason and make us more spontaneous, slightly dangerous. I am thinking of a forty-eight-year-old married woman who was out of her mind with infatuation for her thirty-four-year-old house painter. This woman, a name most everyone in Washington knows, would call into her office sick so she could sit on the floor beside her handyman and watch him roll color up and down her walls. Meeting him marked the first time since her early menopause she felt like having sex. When the handyman didn't respond to her advances, she went to New York City to visit an old boyfriend and had an affair, something she doesn't regret one bit.

"I'm married to a nice man, but the passion part of me isn't fulfilled," she told me. "And so I met up with this man I used to date and he said, 'I want to sleep with you,' and I said, 'Let's go.' I mean, there is this wild and crazy side of me that has been unleashed because of my crush on the house painter. He made me feel beautiful and young and sexy—for the first time in ten years.

"And so this old boyfriend and I made passionate love for four hours in his penthouse apartment," she continues. "It was great. I needed it and he knew I needed it. It was emancipating. I am forty-eight, in a tired marriage, and I need to be reminded that I am still desirable. When I got back, I actually started working with my husband on trying to improve our sexual relationship. I think sex in a marriage is important, and that's what's missing."

Naming no names, but tossing my husband highlights of some of my interviews with wives, Chuck looked at me funny, squinted his disdain, buttered his bagel, then muttered, "Women are dogs." I tell him that men and women are both animals in love; that love itself is bizarre and incomprehensible, that nothing, anymore, is shocking.

We've all heard so many stories of illicit dalliances that there is little that could still shake us up. We are, after all, the jaded generation who elected the rascal boomer President Clinton, who has one very bizarre marriage himself, complete with lying and cheating and almost getting away with it. Our response to Bill Clinton's hound-dogging in the Oval Office, an office that presidents past would not enter without a jacket and tie, was to nod and to wink, even pat him on the back. If President Clinton would have run for a third term, this, before his questionable pardons—he would be elected again, probably, by a wide, worshipful margin.

The former president of the United States is one of us: how can we condemn him? We are a generation prone to sinning and forgiving, a generation driven by guilt and a sense that we are entitled to salvation.

We deal with affairs more with a shrug than a sense of outrage, or even mild unease. Sex scandals with politicians? Please pass the popcorn and change the channel. Many marriages in Washington resemble marriage in Hollywood, a walk-on, walk-off scene in a movie.

The most insightful Washington political writer I know, Evan Thomas, routinely reports on the sordid and sneaky liaisons that go on among politicians and other Capitol powerhouses. Thomas, the assistant managing editor of *Newsweek* magazine, was one of the chief muckrakers responsible for unraveling the dirty details in President Clinton's affair with former White House intern Monica Lewinsky. Married for twenty-five years himself, and the father of two teenage daughters, Thomas has this to say about the institution he has keenly observed:

"You never really know what's going on in another person's marriage. We often think we do and gossip about it, and sometimes we know what drives people apart—infidelity, alcohol, a family crisis. But we don't really know what holds people together. And I think that's good. It shows the complexity and depth of marriage; that it can't be trivialized and easily reduced to pop psychology. Getting married and having a family is the most profound thing we do, and if it isn't, it doesn't last."

We began to view marriage as more fleeting than profound a quarter of a century ago, with the onset of the zipless sex with strangers romanticized by Erica Jong in her 1975 book *Fear of Flying*. Too many of us slept with people we did not love, people we did not even like that much. Loose and lusty, ours is the era that birthed open marriage and cheap, accessible birth control. Sex wasn't for marriage, sex was for fun. Marital commitment started meaning not "for as long as we live," but "for as long as we feel like staying together." Feeling happy became more important than feeling stuck. But as this husband in a midlife slump found out, breaking loose doesn't mean you get to be happy either.

Clark is forty-five, and recently moved out of his marriage of twenty-three years into a house across town. He surrendered in the end not to a sense of duty toward his three children, ages sixteen, eleven, and nine, which for him was always great, but to his own vast loneliness. His decision was expedited by the fact that he met someone else.

Over the years, Clark has complained that his was a marriage with no spark, no love. He said that he and his wife slept in separate bedrooms, and never inquired about each other's work. I've heard identical descriptions from many people who choose to leave marriages—no talking, no touching, no sex, no fun. A professor I've worked with for many years said of her deposed husband: "I didn't want to touch him. I didn't want him to touch me. I crossed through a lead door, sort of like the *Star Trek* air-locked door." Those who spoke to me about leaving unsatisfying marriages most often get up the courage "to pull the trigger," as this professor put it, when they have another set of arms to fall into.

I believe Clark as he tells me his new woman is someone he feels he can't live without, that he feels "doomed" with his wife. I know he speaks the truth when he says it is thrilling to fall in love again, we all know that. But I also know another truth from too many spouses who have been there; that a dark, old shroud perpetually hangs over the shining, new love. Having broken up his family, Clark knows he can never be 100 percent happy. Not that any of us ever are wholly happy, but it is more difficult when you must hurt loved ones to help yourself. This man is understandably a wreck.

He is gaunt from a twenty-pound weight loss, his face is puffed from too much scotch. His wife has been begging him to come back, promising things will be different. Clark asked me what I thought he should do. I told him about the abysses in my own marriage and that what has always resurrected me was the simple knowing that I was in love with my husband. And that, at this point in our lives, as parents to four young children, we needed to be a team operating out of the same headquarters, to effectively run what feels like a boot camp.

Clark said he was not in love with his wife. I asked him if he still felt even a shard of love, as he recalled the early embers of romance that made him fall for her in the first place. And that if he did, he should go home and fan the embers, that the pain he felt about marriage may be nothing compared to the pain he may feel once he's really cut off from his family.

He said nothing for a while, looking pale and old. When he finally spoke, his words came out in a hoarse whisper: "I can't go back to that marriage."

This man is free to go forward and marry another, undeterred by a judgmental society that believes in the absolute sanctity of marriage, as our culture once did. Often when I listen to my journalism students at American University talk about marriage, I feel that they know something we did not when we were inhabitants of the social laboratory of the late 1960s and early 1970s. What I hear from many young men and women entering their twenties is that their parents got it wrong, and they are determined to get it right. They are willing to work harder at relationships; they want marriages that last.

I'm looking at a recent *Time* magazine cover that pictures the four buffed stars of HBO's wildly successful *Sex and the City*, women who talk dirtier and have more sex than anyone I have ever met. And here is my immediate response: What horrible role models for young people. Front and center is Sarah Jessica Parker's character Carrie, with her tumble of hair, perfectly highlighted and curled, falling to breasts encased in a white strapless gown. Her lips are glossed into an iridescent purple pout.

Decked out for an evening of prowling, the *Sex and the City* sirens are a tease for a story on "Who Needs a Husband?" that points to this growing trend: "More women are saying no to marriage and embracing the single life. Are they happy?"

There is much information presented in the *Time* article that attempts to bolster the overarching premise that "single women have come into their own." In 1963, 83 percent of women twenty-five to fifty-five were married; by 1997 that figure had dropped to 65 percent. The 1999 results of long-term research is cited, conducted by the National Marriage Project at Rutgers University, in which marriage rates were found to have plummeted to a forty-year low. We read quote after quote from euphoric single women with good jobs, good looks, even good boyfriends, all expressing the same sentiment: Our own lives are full and free; why do we need to get married?

I flip from the story back to the photo of the four stars of

Sex and the City, in come-hither costumes and stiff coiffures, and stumble again on this cover line: "Are they happy?" *Happy* is not among the first words that come to mind. They are stunning on the outside, but they do not exude real joy from within, and anyone who has been dating too long and too much can tell you why: Sex in the city feels good for fleeting moments, but it's no ticket to a satisfaction that endures. And therein lies the ancient reason why 90 percent of Americans still choose to get married. Being single is lonely. Humans need long-term companionship.

The unhitched women of marrying age catting around big cities in sensational garb aren't usually doing so to "embrace the single life." The purpose of that ritual, quite simply, is to attract a mate so they can stop having to hang around smoky bars with their girlfriends. Most women don't want intimacy on the fly with a fleet of lovers. Most women want to finally find a partner who looks beyond the bottle-gold fibers of highlighted hair and into the fiber of their being. Most women want to be able to skip shaving their legs once in a while and still feel beautiful in the eyes of their men.

Despite new and sobering statistics on the decline in marriage, lots of New Age women want what their mothers and grandmothers wanted—loyal spouses, children, houses with gardens. Many enlightened and hip women, including Sarah Jessica Parker, wife of Matthew Broderick, have discovered that being single is not that fabulous after all.

Most women want fidelity in a partner. They find more fulfillment in a predictable routine, however grinding it can become, than in the quick hits of ecstasy and inevitable agony that comes with dating around. Even Gloria Steinem surrendered to the archaic tradition she has often dismissed as a destructive force to women's rights. "I am happy and surprised," admitted the feminist matriarch when she recently got married for the first time at the age of sixty-six. Steinem, the co-founder of *Ms.* magazine, was wed to entrepreneur David Bale, sixty-one, in September of 2000, in a sunrise ceremony in rural Oklahoma.

Who needs a husband? More people than are willing to admit. People are happiest when they are anchored in a family. People are happiest when they are connected with someone they love, and if they don't feel that need, they are generally in therapy to find out why. Yet, making the leap for young people is a bold act of faith, having grown up trying to heal from their own parents' botched marriages.

I frequently assign my students to write a personal essay on "the most important thing that has ever happened in your life, for better or for worse." Responses range in severity from getting bad acne while spending a semester abroad in Italy to losing a brother to AIDS. The most frequent comeback, however, is recovery from divorce. These college kids express an unwavering desire to be smarter about marriage than their parents' culture.

I just got off the telephone with a former student, Allegra Gatti, twenty-four, who told me she is in love for the first time in her life. She lives in Manhattan, the setting for *Sex and the City*, where she works at a sports club on the Upper West Side, a place filled with lots of singles who are looking to meet somebody while swearing they love being single. Although Gatti's own parents are divorced and so are her boyfriend's, the couple is talking about creating a life together. She is hopeful, not fearful.

"I'm not going to make the same mistake my parents made," Gatti says. "I often wonder if they could still be married if they had recognized what it was they wanted to accomplish together and were willing to do the work. I know that in my own marriage, I'm going to figure out how to keep doing that work. I want to spend my life with someone else, I know that for a fact. It's crazy to think you can be really happy living alone."

Bruce Lustig, the senior rabbi at Washington Hebrew Congregation in Washington, D.C., will not perform a marriage ceremony unless the couple has gone through several counseling sessions with him. It is in these meetings that young people address ways to move through those central issues that Gatti saw her own parents hit as a roadblock.

"One of the difficulties in marriage today is that we live in a disposable society," Lustig starts out. "Your Walkman breaks, you don't fix it, you buy a new one. Your toaster oven breaks, you get a new one. And that mentality transfers over to our relationships. We are often not willing to work at some very simple issues, and when a marriage gets broken—we toss it.

"When I'm talking to young people considering making a commitment to marriage, we talk a lot about bumps to expect on the road," Lustig continues. "I tell them that they can look toward the outside and try to bolt, to escape things that aren't good at the moment. Or they can keep their eyes focused on the relationship they are in and work at making it better."

My own husband is sitting at the kitchen table, dressed in the tattered blue bathrobe I gave him a decade ago, a sight that is comforting and familiar. I am "happy and surprised," in Gloria Steinem's words, that Chuck and I are still married. And proud. We are fully aware of the weight of our accomplishment. We have resisted the numerous urges we've both had to bolt. Am I happy? Generally. Are the singles I know happy, unencumbered and free? Only when what they find during a night on the prowl leads not to sex in the city, but to companionship they can count on.

Many of us who grew up in a posthippie haze of free love are now living with some regret. We realize that having too much superficial love over time can cause an inability to recognize, and honor, the real thing when it comes along. And with this deficiency in handling long-term love, we have created mayhem in the structure of the American family. I have shocked myself, a liberal, in my response to the members of the religious right who say that sex should only be for marriage. I am starting to think they may have a point.

Ann Burmeister was a virgin of twenty-two when she become the wife of David Oettel last summer. An angelic-looking blonde with lustrous skin, she is the daughter of a Lutheran minister in Minnesota. She grew up hearing that flesh should be joined with flesh only after a marriage ceremony has been performed, and that living together is flat-out wrong. While her beliefs go against the main current of contemporary sexuality, Ann has some head-turning takes on the merits of holding out before marriage.

I remember my parents saying to me from the age I understood what sex was about that sex was for marriage, that it was totally, morally wrong outside of marriage. I dated a lot of people and there were pressures to be physical, but I always had that ancient rule from the Bible ingrained in me. I believe basically that premarital sex is a sin, and that God looks at it that way.

I see the damage it has done to my girlfriends who have had multiple sex partners. They go into sex not understanding the bond that takes place when two people make love. It just affects so many different areas. It affects your body, your mind, your soul; your heart gets broken. I know a lot of people who have lots of regrets today; they wish they would have waited at least to have the first person be someone they love. I know that most of the problems in marriage my father sees as a pastor, you can always find a root dealing with sex. As the Bible says, "When the two become one flesh that is not meant to be broken." And when you become one flesh with many people and don't stay with any of them, of course you are going to have problems forming per-

manent unions. When my girlfriends look at me and say, "How can you hold out," I tell them, "How can you not?"

Sex is so intimate. Why would you think of wasting it on just anybody? No wonder there are so many young people who feel so worthless and used at a young age. No wonder there is so much depression among college students. Too much sex is a bad thing. When you become one flesh with a lot of people, it's like ripping a little piece off yourself every time. God's design is for two to become one flesh, not twelve or twenty-five or 100 to become one flesh. That can only lead to a lifetime of pain.

Unfortunately, many marriages don't hold up to Ann's biblical ideal of one flesh and holy covenant. Nor do they resemble the seemingly unshakable partnerships we remember between our own mothers and fathers, most of whom stuck it out until someone died. Marriage today can be fluid, untamed, scary. Those who make it are those with a high threshold for change, challenge, and pain.

As pop philosopher Jacob Needleman writes in *A Little Book on Love*, we inhabit an era when the values of our ancestors no longer shape our expectations or our destinies: "This seems especially so in matters of love," Needleman says. "To honor one's promise or to break it; to hold on to a relationship or to cut oneself free—neither alternative in the long run seems obviously better than the other.

"Look around us," Needleman continues. "Who is happy—over the long run—in their relationships, in their loves? The broken heart is almost everywhere."

When many of us entered marriage, we were professionals in our thirties, not alabaster-skinned coeds like Ann Burmeister Oettel, fresh from dormitories. We already had experienced broken hearts and shattered dreams; we knew you could become one flesh with someone one day and be on your own the next. Beneath the white silk and lace gowns cascading down the aisles were plenty of hardened hearts and toughened hides. Few were falling for the antiquated promise that two people can actually become one—modern marriages are frequently the melding of two defiant and experienced individuals who retain two last names, two bank accounts, separate lives.

When Ted Turner jokingly suggested that perhaps the "no adultery" rule should be scratched from the Ten Commandments, I heard a lot of people agree, with a weary shrug, that he might have a point. Later, Turner and Jane Fonda, the golden couple who sizzled with possibility and sexuality, would split, and while this was not a shock, it was another sad defeat for the happily-ever-after myth. Nothing is guaranteed to be forever, even for partners who are drawn together as alleged soul mates like Ted and Jane, who seemed so right, who could have been, should have been, but were not to be. Last heard, he is with another woman. And Jane Fonda, thrice-married and sixty-two, is quoted in a recent *Good Housekeeping* interview with writer Joanna Powell as realizing she finally understands what she needs to do in love:

"After I turned sixty I began to own my voice, own my power. . . . There is no reason for a woman to give up her soul in order to please a man."

Yet, even the most well-meaning of spouses are not immune to adulterous impulses, felt by them or by their partners. While it is destructive, hurtful, and wrong, the truth is that lots of women and men screw around outside of marriage; you know them and I know them, and I hear of more every day. Some stay married, some marry the person who caused them to stray, some end up tortured and alone. But no one escapes being somehow leeched, forever, by the affair's poisonous wake.

A Washington circuit court judge of forty-five was so scarred when her marriage fell apart seven years ago because of her husband's affair that she has vowed never to marry again. Never. This, even though she knows that a marriage can last and be good—her parents have been together for fifty years—and she is living with a man who is loving and kind and committed. Here is her story.

I was absolutely in love with my husband, but he would complain that I never found the right way to balance my work and children and make him a part of my life. And he was right in a way; but I was very much in love with him. Then I became very in love with my daughters.

When I got married, I expected a life of partnership, I thought he would take care of me and I would take care of him. I thought together we would nurture and raise our children. It wasn't only the fidelity, it was a myriad of issues. When I found out he was being unfaithful, the reason it took me so long to leave him was not because I wanted to save the marriage, but I had children, a six-month-old baby and a two-year-old, and I was very much afraid to go on alone.

Then I met a white knight at work who listened and offered comfort when we finally did go through the divorce, and the huge custody battle. And we developed a relationship that is still going strong after many years. It's a passionate, very romantic relationship. It's not a relationship based on problem solving or daily needs. My daughters visit their father every other weekend; my lover's kids are grown, and we are able to spend a lot of time just the two of us alone. He is absolutely my soul mate, he can read me, he can read my face, he absolutely wants to know what's going on inside of my head. It's amazing.

But you know, before my husband and I had children, there was a great deal of richness, there was a lot of love in our relationship. And then, bang, he was out of there. It made me realize that in a nonblood relationship, people can wake up in the morn-

ing and say, "I don't love you anymore," then leave. And since I once gave everything in a marriage, I believe that's what would happen if I got married again—I would give everything. So now, although this other man and I now live together, own a house together, we are monogamously committed to one another, not being his wife feels safer. I understand that I'm on this side of the line. If he gets up in the morning and says, "Listen, it's been great, but I really need to move on," I can live with it. I'll survive that. If I got married and that happened again, I'm not sure I could.

I am talking now to a man in Chicago on the telephone, and can barely hear him because one of his children, a seven-year-old girl, is crying in the background. The demise of his marriage followed the same plot line as the one above: His wife fell out of love with him, met someone else, and wanted out, five children later. He laughed bitterly as his daughter continued to wail.

"This happens every Sunday," says the man, a thirty-nine-year-old mortgage banker. "The kids are with me weekends, and they hate having to pack up and leave this house, the house where they grew up, and go spend half the week in a strange apartment, without me. My daughter said to me the other day, 'Daddy, I hate being divorced. When is this going to stop?'

"She's too young for me to tell her that this isn't going to stop. She still has hope. What am I going to say? That after twenty years, her mother decided she didn't love me anymore, and that this family unit as she knew it, with a mommy and daddy who lived together, from now on will always be a patchwork, with pieces strewn everywhere.

"Up until the end, I would have stayed married," this man continues. "Even with my wife telling me that she didn't love me. I could have lived with that; I mean, we have five children together. But my wife couldn't do it."

WHAT'S LOVE GOT TO DO WITH IT?

I am having lunch with my wise, wry friend Susan at Cactus Cantina in Washington, D.C. The day is cold and rainy and we are drinking frozen margaritas and eating hot *chili con queso*. I am telling her about all these people I knew whose marriages were eviscerating because someone fell out of love. Susan stops eating and drinking and says in a stony voice: "Not being in love is not a good enough reason to leave a marriage, especially when there are children." We continue a conversation about the importance of being madly in love in a marriage, weighed up against other factors, such as having someone who is loyal and dependable.

After ten years of marriage, a union that has produced a six-year-old daughter and an eight-year-old son, here are some of Susan's insights:

I think love takes on different life forms at different stages. Love, in essence, is sequential. Some days, love can be a powerful and overwhelming force—tempestuous, exhilarating. Then, if you are lucky, love can become calm and settling. Love changes. That's a good thing. Anyone who thinks that kind of high intensity lasts hasn't been in enough long relationships.

I went into my marriage, at age thirty-seven, believing I had found someone with whom I could juggle the fragility of life. Not someone with whom I thought I would have a life of passionate sex. Marriage has great limitations. That's why God created flirting. For me, my expectations of marriage are limited to: 1) Are our life's goals relatively similar?; 2) Is he a good father?; 3) Can we support each other through the bad times?; and 4) Will he share responsibility for all the shit that needs to be done? Anything else above that is gravy.

Before, for many years, I had too many sexual partners to count, lived fascinating lives with some great men, none of whom I'd ever think of marrying. Because, in the end, they couldn't deal with what I knew life would be: One long roller-coaster ride.

After lunch, during the hour-long drive back home, I thought about the glorious feeling we all feel, perhaps we have felt more than once, of being obsessively in love with someone. I flash on the writhing, incandescent, ship-wrecked lovers doing it like starving animals in Lina Wertmuller's film *Swept Away*, . . . her delicate fingers seemingly tearing his skin right to the bone. Although Wertmuller's tale of characters in their carnal explosion in the wilderness was no happily-ever-after story—it was over by the time they were rescued—this man and woman, alone on the sandy lip of an island, are a prickly reminder of the lyrical and erotic variations one life can resonate in, and how most people are stuck in the middle range.

Donna, a friend from Vermont, recently introduced me to a man who gave her the incentive to leave her middle-range marriage. She says theirs is the best sex she has ever had in her life and she's had lots of it. I met Mr. Bull-In-Bed, and the *Swept Away* musk was pungent as we all drank red wine on the terrace of an Indian restaurant on a summer night.

Donna eventually left her husband, and she now lives with her lover in an apartment that is half the size of her house, which her husband got in the divorce. Sex is still great, but there's not as much of it, as these two victims of Cupid, both dot.com executives with frantic lives, have had to deal with the cold reality of fitting in time for romance when also dealing with ex-spouses, six young kids between them, and winding up poor after divorce settlements. Nothing like the grind of reality to take the sizzle out of a libido.

"After ecstasy—the laundry," as that great Buddhist saying goes.

No one among us is above the timeless nature of romantic affection, a force field that inevitably comes and goes in waves. "Love is like a fever which comes and goes quite independently of the will," Stendhal writes in his book *Love*. This frees us from looking toward someone else's relationship as a model to which we feel our own marriage should measure up. Everybody messes up and no one is ever totally honest about what's going on, especially when it comes to sex.

We will never know what is the cementing force between men and women who are not us, not even our mothers and fathers or our sisters and brothers. We only see people when they are putting on their public faces; we do not see them when they are in their bedrooms saying and doing God knows what. So don't even try to understand why some marriages that are outwardly horrid last and last. The only thing we can know for sure is that everyone married suffers to some degree, but to what degree, we'll never know.

These truths about marriage are both emancipating and depressing. Emancipating because we no longer have to feel like the grass is greener on the other side; everyone has lawns with brown patches, spots that are parched. But the truth is depressing because the ancient institution which was designed to be the most sacred and transcendent of bonds between humans has turned out to be as fragile and flawed as the rest of our lives.

No one would expect the passengers on the Magical Mystery Tour to float docilely to the ground and surrender to real marriage in real life, with needy kids, too many bills, too little time. Those needy kids are now reflecting hard on ways to lead a marriage renaissance and not perpetuate the divorce revolution their own parents started.

It is not easy to be more hopeful than cynical. Over the thirteen years that I've been teaching college, I have heard students grow more adamant in their desire to be in a long-term love, but increasingly doubtful about finding it, this from living through the splits and remarriages and resplits between their own parents, parents' friends, uncles, and aunts. They have seen the marriages of many of their heros dissipate, from Harrison Ford to Nelson Mandela. They cannot rely on social forces to propel them toward marriage and parenthood; no longer does one have to wear the proper title of husband or wife to have a baby. Nor can they count on moral messengers to help hold the relationship together; much of the clergy that once warned parishioners they would fry in hell for divorce has backed down considerably.

While there are virginal newlyweds like Ann Burmeister Oettel who still believe that a walk down the aisle means a stroll into eternity, most young people today are suspicious and painfully realistic. They come to this place honestly; many grew up in homes watching parents behave like ridiculous, selfish children.

Marie is a senior at the University of Arizona whose parents had what she calls a "crazy, crazy marriage." She repeatedly twirls the bottom of the turquoise T-shirt that has popped out of her blue jeans as she talks about what went on at home:

My mom and dad have separated and gotten back together seven times, and I have grown up watching a totally loveless marriage. There was infidelity. My dad's last girlfriend was twenty-nine. She was his former secretary, and she had two very small children.

When I was young, we lived outside of Chicago and our next door neighbor's daughter and I were best friends. Her mother and my father had an affair for a long time, and we all knew about it; even my mom knew about it. They moved to another suburb and he would take my sister and I to go visit her. And he would say to us, "Now, make sure you tell your mom we went to Kiddie Land," instead of what we were really doing. He also had other girlfriends; we met them all.

My dad is fifty-one, but really he has always acted like a little kid. When I was nine years old, he moved out of our house and went to live with his old girlfriend, the mother of my best friend. He moved out on my mom's birthday, if you can believe it. This woman had left her husband, and her two kids were living with her. I just found out this recently, but my friend used to call my father "Daddy." He used to buy her clothes and things, and really treat her just like a daughter. Then one day, out of the blue, he moved back home, and told us that he was never going to do that to us again, that he and his lady friend were absolutely through. A few years later, we moved as a family to Phoenix.

By the time I was a freshman in college, I had a serious boyfriend. But I was having some real problems with the relationship. I just couldn't trust him, I couldn't believe him. When he woke up to leave the dorm, I would go through his drawers, looking for hair clips, stray phone numbers, snooping around his letters. I didn't have any reason to be suspicious, but I thought that's how you are supposed to be in a relationship. And we ended up breaking up.

My mom said, "Marie, you can't be like that. You're going to ruin every relationship you're in if you do that." My sister used to do the same thing, and she'd pick fights with her boyfriend. One day she yelled at my mom and said, "This is all your fault that we're not getting along with our boyfriends. That's how we saw you treat Dad."

After not seeing her for eleven years, recently my dad called his old girlfriend in Chicago again. The next thing we know, she is moving to Phoenix to be with him. Her kids are in their twenties now, so she figured, "What the hell?" Here's the strangest part—after years and years of all this, my parents still weren't divorced.

That's some of the story of my dysfunctional family. This will surprise you: I still can't wait to get married. Not now, but in seven or eight years. I want to have a huge wedding and a huge gown and get married in a beautiful place with hundreds of people to a man whom I deeply love, to my soul mate. Of course, I fear divorce, everybody should fear divorce today. But I also know I'm going to work harder on my marriage than anyone you have ever seen. I do not want to end up like my parents; they are both really great people, but they never had a real marriage together. It's been a circus.

But even all those times my parents weren't living together, I didn't feel strange about it, because it was like everybody's parents I knew were divorced or separated. It was almost the in thing, for your parents not to be together. So it was like, I'm just like everybody else. Divorce was no big deal. Remarriage was no big deal.

But now that I'm older, I do think marriage is a big deal; marriage should be built on trust, on making a promise. Growing up, I saw my mom crying a lot; I don't want my kids to see me that way. I want something better than what my parents had.

I look at my father now, and he says he's with the love of his life, the Chicago woman. But they never dated like you do in a real relationship. They've spent their whole time together sneaking around other people's backs. Now they are getting married. We'll see what happens.

I think of my own parents, who loved and laughed and fought and stayed married, of a mother who didn't work and of a father who worked constantly, building Marvel Metal, his

Chicago-based office furniture company. They struck many bumps and pits along the way, raising three children close in age, yet they would never have thought of splitting up or even going into counseling. Nor would have any of their close friends, all of whom stuck it out, and didn't have the cultural compulsion to obsess over the quality of their relationships. Back then, therapy was for patients in insane asylums.

Marriage was marriage, private and personal, not something you took into the shop, like a car or a vacuum cleaner to get fussed over and fixed by someone else. Twined by grit, habit, children, and faith, my mother and father stayed together for thirty-four years, working it out on their own without a therapist's directives and separating only after my father died in 1986. I can think of only one friend of mine at Horace Mann elementary school in largely Catholic Oak Park, Illinois, whose parents had divorced.

Most of our parents were wary of straying from their safe routines into the unknown. When adultery was discovered, it seldom dissolved a marriage. People actually followed this dictum from God in the book of Corinthians: "A husband must not divorce his wife." Our parents stayed married because they were supposed to, those were the rules. They never had the time or the inclination to indulge in the luxury of pondering their happiness or retreating to Esalen to take workshops like one offered recently called the Hindu Path of Bliss.

Growing up poor in the Depression, they were consumed with tangible destinations, like figuring out how to afford college educations for us. Their affluent offspring are consumed with cosmic adventures such as trying to repair present lives by channeling past lives through angels and psychics. Generations past put one foot in front of the other just to get by, toiling ruthlessly at their jobs to give their children lives dramatically better than their own.

When my parents got married in 1952, Dwight D. Eisenhower was president and married to sweet-faced Mamie with the bangs. In postwar America, families were searing beef in their backyards with no talk about charred meats containing fats and carcinogens. Wives had stiff flips and drawers full of girdles and fat babies at home. They weren't whining over how to balance career and kids, even though many of them were secretly having silent, screaming breakdowns from what Betty Friedan called "the trapped housewife syndrome" in her 1962 book *The Feminine Mystique*, which sparked the modern feminist movement. This era glorified child rearing and homemaking as the ultimate fruition of femininity and ostracized women who felt differently.

"Women who . . . had trouble adjusting to creative homemaking were labeled neurotic, perverted, or schizophrenic," writes Stephanie Coontz in *The Way We Never Were*, a book that reveals the warts that were camouflaged behind the creamy midcentury veneer. Coontz cites a study of women believed to be schizophrenic in the San Francisco Bay Area during the 1950s who were subjected to institutionalization and electric-shock treatments to force them to embrace their domestic roles and subservience to their husbands.

"Beneath the polished facades of many 'ideal' families, suburban as well as urban, was violence, terror, or simply grinding misery that only occasionally came to light," notes Coontz.

If the wives allowed the "grinding misery" to come to light they would have rocked the outwardly placid families from which they drew their central source of identity and security. The malaise, which was most likely prevalent in the marriages of the 1950s, was shielded from the neighbors' eyes; the boom of babies born during that repressed era turned out to be quite the opposite—exhibitionists with no scruples.

Today, frank sexuality, from penile dysfunction to oral sex, is routine dinner conversation and fodder for stories sung by a giddy chorus of journalists to a public that devours every word, all the while complaining how sick they are of the filth they read in the newspaper and hear on TV. Yet, there were plenty of tawdry truths behind the fab fifties fantasy, but they weren't discussed in the news or in living rooms. There was no sex scandal ricocheting through the White House— although there could have been a few had the media been like they are today, relentless, like dogs chewing through bones.

During his days as a general in World War II, bald, benign Ike Eisenhower was allegedly fooling around with his beautiful personal assistant and driver, a young Irishwoman named Kay Summersby, while First Lady Mamie stewed about the rumors and played a lot of bridge back home. Who could imagine that Dwight D. Eisenhower would have made anyone feel the way Summersby says he did in her 1976 autobiography, *Past Forgetting: My Love Affair with Dwight D. Eisenhower.*

"It was like an explosion," writes Summersby. "We were suddenly in each other's arms. His kisses absolutely unraveled me. Hungry, strong, demanding. And I responded every bit as passionately. He stopped, took my face between his hands. 'Goddamn it,' he said. 'I love you.' We were breathing as if we had run up a dozen flights of stairs."

By 1976, when Summersby tattled in her memoir, Americans hardly blinked, having already caught many powerful men in the arms of their babes, and in their lies. The naughty side of clean-cut Ike was nothing compared to the trouble we had seen, from the herd claiming they, too, had slept with President Kennedy to the resignation in disgrace of President Nixon that sent his top White House henchmen to prison. By the year 2001, there's virtually nothing we haven't seen, and little that surprises us.

We've witnessed President Clinton stripped down and naked; it made us strip away our own pretenses at having any kind of perfect marriage, or perfect life. Any explosion of presidential peccadilloes erupting in prime-time blasts during the 1950s would have meant that those pristine families in their suburban enclaves would have had to face the truths that we are now facing. Our parents would have had to look beyond the superficial to the awful, real stuff simmering below the surface, stuff that could gush out at any moment, like unstoppable geysers. That would have shattered what Plato called their "world of appearances."

Today, there are no appearances. When the marriage of the most prominent couple in America started straining, popping buttons, ripping at the seams—before our eyes, blow by blow, round the clock, for more than a year—the fairy-tale myths about marriage were irrevocably stretched, contorted, changed. We were sad and outraged at a nubile, shrewd White House intern and our bad-boy president who couldn't resist her flick of the thong, but as a result perhaps less desperate to hide our own vulnerability and the scars in our own imperfect unions.

When President Clinton's stained laundry was hung out for the world to see, we were all humbled and ashamed, even afraid—who would be next to get caught? He is emblematic of our generation, a man-child who wants it both ways. Clinton's approval ratings never dramatically fluctuated. Yet, the flaws and travails of this baby boomer president and his steely first lady were a mirror shoved in our faces, broken into shards of shattered illusions on monogamy and commitment and staying happy with one person in one house for one, entire life.

What will happen to Hillary and Bill Clinton's marriage nobody knows, probably not even them. What will happen to your marriage? Do you know, for certain? Although I am hopeful that my marriage, which began in a Chicago snowstorm, will endure, there are no guarantees, for me or for anyone who has embarked upon a love relationship. All we can do to tip the scales is work hard every day, on ourselves, on being more grateful, more tolerant. I believe in the cliché that you take your baggage with you, and that another person cannot make you happy, you must do that for yourself. Yet, even for the most devoted of spouses, the curse and blessing of being curious and in middle age and capable of living another half century is that in the decades to come there lies a staggering amount of choices in life.

The most recent figure for divorce in the United States sits right at 49 percent of all marriages. Despite this dreary fact, most Americans are still getting married with big dreams, in big dresses, in lavish settings, generating an estimated $32 billion in annual retail sales. And even if surveys show the under-thirty set are skittish, more than 90 percent of all men and women in our country do, at some point, become brides and grooms.

I spoke to Millie Martini Bratten, the longtime editor of *Brides* magazine, about a recent survey conducted by her magazine in which 68 percent of readers indicated that they had the wedding they dreamed of since childhood.

"Even though today's bride and groom are older and wiser, the hope and excitement about the wedding and getting married is still there," Bratten said. "That means having a big, traditional wedding surrounded by family and friends, and saying time-honored vows—most often in a religious setting. There is still that feeling that a wedding is a major life event, that they are committing to one another for a lifetime.

"What is different today is that people now know that a good marriage doesn't just happen by itself," added Bratten. "I've been at *Brides* for twenty-three years, and our editorials have evolved to project and reflect the excitement of marriage, yet at the same time address the anxiety issues—of in-laws, of the fact that he is not perfect and neither are you, of second marriages, of money. We hear from a lot of people who say, 'I saw my parents' marriage fall apart, I want to know what *not* to do.' There is a lot more realism about what is required to live together until death us do part—which with increased longevity, is far longer than it used to be."

The Choice

On the one hand, I want to tell my friends-in-lust that infatuation inevitably withers, that all it will take is a month of sharing a bathroom for the ecstasy to subside.
On the other hand, I want their lives.

When my childhood friend Liza, introduced briefly earlier, called from Colorado to announce she was leaving her long marriage to be with Mr. Hubba-Hubba, a world-class runner and A-plus lover, I distinctly recalled the night in 1977 when I was a bridesmaid at her big wedding in a big hotel ballroom in St. Louis. Back then, she was hopeful she had a stab at a forever marriage by picking this husband, a cardiologist, successful, an impeccable computer match. And now, almost twenty years later, she was leaving that marriage she considered good, but never great, for a man she considered extraordinary. I thought of the great dress I wore as her bridesmaid, a champagne swirl of silk with a cowl neck and asymmetrical hemline, a gown that still hangs in my mother's closet to go to a grand-daughter someday.

Liza was the first friend of mine to get married and the first friend to have a baby. She seemed to thrive as a wife who didn't work, tended a baby girl, and made dinner for her husband every night. But that was her veneer. Now she is telling me that inside she was "asleep." Always slim and athletic, with thick, black hair and startling green eyes, Liza says that since meeting this man, she is in the best shape she had ever been in, body and mind. Here is her story:

The problem with my marriage was always suppressing my-self, always compromising. A couple of years after our daughter was born I got pregnant again, but my husband did not want any more kids, and even though I didn't want an abortion, I didn't feel that I could stand up and say no. I am not blaming him for this; I had unconsciously accepted a subordinate role. I got pregnant again when I was forty; by that time my daughter was an adolescent, and I had another abortion which I didn't want to get. But my husband absolutely didn't want any more children. He felt that we did such a good job the first time around, he didn't want to take the chance of having a difficult second child.

So I basically squashed my feelings of anger about the abortions, or about anything, because he always had this unwavering certainty about things. I was attracted to his supreme confidence and clarity because it was something I didn't have.

He was a cardiologist and he told me right away I didn't have to work, he could afford to support me, and I loved that, again, that confidence. It was hard at the beginning of our marriage when he would show this unshakable will because I would respond by suppressing myself, because I didn't want him to be angry. And so I didn't stand up to him when things bothered me.

He left his practice and we moved from St. Louis to Colorado so he could follow new career paths as a consultant to a corporation in Denver. Once we got there, he did not like to go on weekend excursions. So my daughter became my mate on getaways to Boulder, Colorado Springs, Vail. I never went anywhere with my husband. Yet, I didn't feel lonely; I would rationalize it like this: You can't expect everything from one person. I'll just go out and have lunch with friends since my husband doesn't like to go to restaurants. I'll go for walks with friends since my husband doesn't like the outdoors.

He did make me feel taken care of in terms of security, especially financial, and there was an emotional security, too, because he was very expressive about his love for me. But my adventurous, playful, spiritual side was totally undeveloped. He eventually left his consulting job because the stress level put him into a depression. He started a business that wasn't successful. When that business shut down, I took a job with a nonprofit organization. And that's where and when I met this other man, John, a champion runner.

I really got to know John in Los Angeles, where we were participating in a twenty-six-mile marathon. I went to L.A. alone because my husband didn't like flying. I remember noticing John the day after the marathon and a group of us went to the beach, getting our last bit of sun. I asked him about his personal life, about his wife, why she wasn't there, and he told me she didn't like to go places. I told him my husband didn't, either. The night before, I had a dream that John and I had been making out and here we were talking, and I felt very sexy.

I thought he was handsome and nice, but here I was in an eighteen-year-old marriage with a sixteen-year-old daughter, seemingly very content and happy. I wasn't looking to find somebody else. But John and I resumed our friendship when we returned to Colorado. We had another marathon coming up in Seattle, and we started talking about organizing a side trip to go rafting. My husband knew all about it, even though it was a little odd that I was planning a vacation with another man. I asked him, "Do you have a problem with this?" His answer was: "As long as you don't sleep with him I don't care what you do."

After the Seattle marathon, when I crossed the finish line, it was one of those Personal Best moments. I was higher than a kite and I hugged John. That night, after dinner with a group, John and I went off to this sunken room off the side of the bar. I asked him all sorts of things about his twenty-year marriage, such as why he didn't have kids. And then I started opening up about myself. We were in that bar until about 2 a.m., in chairs opposite each other, not physically close, but feeling very, very close.

He said that no one had ever been that curious about him,

either. Like me, he had never looked outside his marriage, he had never had an affair, he was a straight arrow. We left the bar, walked back to our hotel, and I knew it was a dangerous moment because he should have turned left to go to his room and I should have turned right to go to my room. But he walked me to my door, and I turned around and we kissed, and this electricity just shot through me.

The next night we had a couple of hours alone, and I was feeling passion, love, infatuated, totally immersed in him. It was the most unbelievable experience. I wanted to be with him every second. And it wasn't even sexual; it was an emotional hunger I didn't know I had. I came back from Seattle very confused. Over the next month and a half we saw each other, and it became clearer to me that our relationship was getting too intimate to be able to maintain and stay married. We spent a lot of time talking about what we should do.

I had to be honest with my husband because the feelings were too overwhelming to lead a secret life with this other man. I wanted to be with John every waking moment. I knew my only option was to move out of our house.

The way I tried to explain it to my husband was that there was something missing in our marriage. He asked me what was missing. I tried to explain, using John as an example, saying this man listens to me. I feel heard. I feel important. My husband looked at me and said, "I think what's happened is you've fallen in love with him." And I said: "Yes." My husband said, "Well, that I can deal with. I can deal with the truth."

I packed my bags and moved into an apartment nearby. Our daughter was a sophomore in high school at the time. I told her I was going through a midlife reevaluation. She was angry with me for disrupting and destroying her family life. And although she did stay with me sometimes, I felt her totally withdraw from me. It was the worst thing imaginable. I tried to draw her out, but she wouldn't talk; it was very painful, a horrible time.

My husband and I went to therapy together three or four times, but I couldn't muster up the commitment to work on our marriage. I was too intrigued about what life could be with John. The therapist said, "If you want to make this marriage work, you are going to have to stop seeing this other man." So I tried for a while because I decided in my own heart that I couldn't live with myself if I hadn't given my marriage a chance.

I moved back home for about six weeks and did not see John. I realized that what I had with my husband wasn't a dead marriage, there were a lot of good things, and I was very confused. I loved my husband. I had been with him almost twenty years, and it was a good life. We had a daughter. We were a family. But as the weeks went by, I realized that what John catalyzed was the part of me that had gone to sleep and was starting to wake up.

I told my husband that I couldn't go back to our marriage. We split up and he bought a condominium a half a mile away. Our daughter reacted coldly; she wasn't emotional, she didn't display anything, which was disturbing. Her grades dropped that year and she wanted nothing to do with John. I was really torn up, but I felt driven, that it was something I had to do.

After my husband and I separated, I could finally see a lot of John, and I started comparing them. I saw that both of these guys were falling short of perfection, neither was 100 percent. What I really wanted to do was blend them together into one person; it would have been the perfect man.

My own parents divorced when I was twenty, a junior in college, and it came as a total shock. I wasn't even aware it had been brewing. My mother called me on a Sunday and said, "By the way, your father moved out." She explained that they had very different interests, and she wasn't happy. When I did the same thing, both of my parents were very supportive, and encouraged me to follow my heart. My father said, "It's okay to change horses in the middle of the race," and I needed to hear that. Yet, it took a long time to actually say to John, "Yes, you are the one," because there were still a lot of feelings for my husband. I was still in shock over this tremendous upheaval.

I had moved out of my house, left my husband, hurt my child, caused all this turmoil for our family. This man had left his own marriage. There still remained a question in my mind whether I was doing the right thing. I still felt so guilty, yet these other feelings were so compelling. John was refreshing, revitalizing. But it was very hard to decide to get married again.

I had this fear of getting trapped and losing myself again by turning myself over to a marriage and to a man. John's feeling was the opposite, that marriage would not be a trap, it would be emancipating. One day, we were having a heated discussion about commitment and he said, "Just marry me." And I said, "Okay." We got married in 1998.

It's been more than two years now, and I don't feel like I did the right thing or I did the wrong thing. I feel like I made a choice, and I knew there would be consequences, as there are every time you take one fork in the road. I went through a very tough process of self-discovery, and I am happy with the choice I made. And I'll never know if I would have been happy with the choice to stay in my old marriage. I remember once dropping our daughter off at my ex-husband's house, and he and I gave each other a little kiss at the door, and it felt good.

Marrying again has had a strange effect. I've learned that there is no perfect match. There's always going to be something that isn't exactly right. With my husband, it was his remoteness and self-centeredness. With John, it's just little quirks, traits that are sometimes irritating because they are odd and unfamiliar. He dabs his runny nose with cloth napkins at restaurants. He wears sweatpants that are really short, and they have two little

holes in the rear end, and he wears them constantly. Inevitably,
comparisons about the two husbands come up every day.

The infatuation stage is over and now has come a settling
into reality and realizing that this new situation isn't some pana-
cea, either. It's like a friend of mine described it: "When you go
and look for a house, you are going to find a house with a fire-
place that doesn't have a great view. Then you are going to find
a house with a great view but it doesn't have a fireplace. There
are always compromises." But there was this driving compulsion,
a hunger that really sparked everything. I felt it was one of those
chances I couldn't turn away from.

Sometimes you need a wake-up call, that's what I've learned
throughout all this. Getting married the first time, at twenty-
three, was like a fairy tale, following along the yellow brick road,
in my mother's footsteps. Over the years, I had fallen asleep.

As for my second marriage, I do see John as a partner for
life, even though it's not perfect. But I do have some regrets as I
look back. It makes me sad that our daughter had to go through
such a painful time. And, after twenty years having it one way,
it takes a long time to establish a new set of routines that feel
familiar. Yet, I can be entirely myself 100 percent of the time in
this marriage. I don't have to edit myself, like I did with my first
husband, who was so demanding, I always had to put him first.
If he didn't want to talk about something, we didn't talk. If he
didn't want to go somewhere, we didn't go.

I'm happy with what I've done, but I can't label the choice
as right or wrong. It's simply the path I took. I made an eyes-
open decision to go in one direction and to deal completely with
whatever consequences came with having made that choice. I feel
like I was in a cocoon and that now I am flying. It is still some-
times scary though, because the cocoon was warm and safe.

I'm thinking about the infatuation phase of love, borne
of lust, the surge that emanates from the loins and unglues

even the most sane and centered of us. It is the burst that makes us fly like Liza, a butterfly set free. Anyone and anything can ignite the lust response—a probing stare, the bones in someone's shoulders, the shape of someone's hands, a question posed that makes you spout forth profound, cathartic sentences. This urgency to unite is wired into our brain chemistry, claims anthropologist Helen Fisher in her book *Anatomy of Love*, a study of adultery, monogamy, and divorce throughout history.

Writes Fisher: "This violent emotional disturbance that we call infatuation (or attraction) may begin with a small molecule called phenylethylamine, or PEA. Known as the excitant amine, PEA is a substance in the brain that causes feelings of elation, exhilaration, and euphoria."

Whether infatuation is induced by chemicals or mystically inspired, once bitten and smitten, we are aflame. The fury of love springs from the soul, and therefore cannot be doused by free will or rationale. We are its victims, not its master. Obsessive love makes us forget everything else, debts, food, sleep. We become spineless, addicted, too often without conscience. The elation that comes with new love opens every pore and electrifies every nerve ending. It's the best damned feeling we've ever felt.

As described by Fisher, "You take foolish risks, say stupid things, laugh too hard, reveal dark secrets, talk all night . . . oblivious to all the world as you tumble through a fever, breathless, etherized by bliss."

Thankfully, it is not a high that is biologically sustainable, as other chemicals kick in and lust turns into attachment. Although attachment, as in growing secure and comfortable with a partner, is not nearly as scintillating as lust. But, who could stand to tingle all the time? Love at that decibel feels more like a ravaging disease that needs to be cured. Fisher puts the normal duration of the infatuation stage as two to three years, and after surveying a pattern in divorce statistics in sixty-two cultures, finds that the peak time for a couple to divorce tends to be in the fourth year of the relationship. Because we are designed to fall in love but not stay that way, we must resist our natural, animal restlessness with the sheer force of our human will power.

We all know people who blindly flit from flower to flower, leaving one love swiftly for another when the rush of infatuation dies. These are desperate folks, not happy folks.

We must remind ourselves that lovers who appear godlike will not stay that way, that when the four-year itch hits we'll be flooded with new brain chemicals that could turn Mr. Dream Machine into a boring schlump. We need to keep remembering that nothing real can ever throb like the psychedelic dance in our imaginations, that fantasy is fantasy, and reality is what's really going on.

I'm thinking of the many people who spoke to me for this book on the experience of fairy dust rapidly disappearing from their eyes, when enough time passed and they began to notice their princes and princesses were really commoners with pimples and problems and fat. In Germaine Greer's *The Female Eunuch,* which helped to articulate the gripes that ignited the feminist movement of the sixties, the author sneers at loving blindly and madly in her chapter called "Obsession." Greer likens being in love to being "in pain, in shock, in trouble."

"The love object occupies the thoughts of the person diagnosed 'in love' all the time, despite the probability that very little is actually known about it," she writes. "Expectations are set up which no human being could fulfill.

"The impotence of will and rationality to deal with this mania is recognized in the common terms *madly, wildly, deliriously, head-over-heels* in love, while it would be oxymoronic to claim to be gently, reliably or sensibly in love."

As a UPI reporter, I had an opportunity to interview Germaine Greer when she came through Washington on a book tour some fifteen years ago. At the time, this sensible skeptic about romantic love told me she had met someone new and she was excited by the possibility of romance. She was wary to trust the pleasure of anticipation she was feeling, but it was there nonetheless. Whether the new person was just a whim, or a partner who would be around for a while, a connection had definitely occurred. And even Greer, the icon of feminism, couldn't escape the flicker of magic and curiosity that occurs when chemistry with another person takes place. No one can; all we can do is to control how we handle it.

"Mystery is critical to romantic love," writes Fisher in *Anatomy of Love*. "Barriers also seem to provoke the madness. The chase. If a person is difficult 'to get,' it piques one's interest. In fact, this element of conquest is often central to infatuation, hence what has become known as the Romeo and Juliet effect: if real impediments exist, as the family feud between Shakespeare's Montagues and Capulets, these obstructions are likely to intensify one's passion. No wonder people fall for an individual who is married, a foreigner, or someone separated from them by an obstacle that appears almost insurmountable."

I still feel that mystery with Chuck; he is my opposite in nearly every way, therefore he remains a stranger, there's always something I can't quite touch, something about him I don't quite get. Lots of people say of their spouse, "I'm married to my best friend" and it's all so cozy and chatty. That's not our house; there's static—and electricity—between us, and it's not a bad thing. Some tension and tumult keeps us on our toes, it keeps us from falling asleep in our marriage.

Research shows that most divorces occur in the first years of marriage. Obviously, it's easier to leave a new marriage, particularly one with no children. But once we get past the tenth anniversary, an aging marriage, even a difficult one, is hard to disassemble, to discard, in the way that worn cowboy boots from college become impossible to throw out. The longer we live, the more history we want surrounding us, like a faded quilt that is frayed, with holes. The quilt may not even keep us warm anymore. But we hold on, for security, for nostalgia. A marriage that's only been around for a couple of years seems less valuable, more disposable. It's not vintage cowboy boots we are parting with; it's more like gently worn clothing taken to a consignment shop, a transaction that makes some people not even cast a backward glance.

"I am shocked by the coolness of some of the couples I see in their late twenties and early thirties who want out," says divorce lawyer Robert Liotta, a man who doesn't shock easily after twenty-five years in Washington, one of the leading divorce towns in America. "It shocks me how unruffled they are when they come in and say, 'I want a divorce.' I am shocked at the lack of heat, the lack of emotion, the lack of anxiety. They don't want to commiserate, they just want the divorce.

"To me, it seems almost like a business deal; I almost regret that they don't feel more pain," continues Liotta. "There is a very casual attitude today among many young professional couples with no kids who don't have joint checking accounts and both work all the time. They call it quits because they really don't see each other, they haven't ever tried to act as a family. They are on parallel tracks but they never come face to face. There is no sadness when they part. The people in their forties and fifties who come in here, most of them cry. The anxiety goes on for months; there is much pain and confusion, and agonizing."

Liotta says that people split for many reasons, including money, incompatibility, boredom. But in his experience helping hundreds of couples through this grueling passage, he finds that it's lack of intimacy, which leads to betrayal, that heads the list of reasons for initiating divorce. It's usually the woman who takes the lead: The most recent broad-scale study on divorce that looked at 46,000 cases showed that more than two-thirds of the people filing were the wives. This clearly points to the postfeminist trend of females not staying in a marriage because they feel like they have to, either for financial support or for self-identity.

Liza from Colorado was honest with her husband that she was in love with another man. You may not agree with what she chose to do, but at least in America we have that choice. Disturbing though the fact may be that our steely pow-erhouse of a country has become a nation known for crumbling marriages, we are fortunate to have freedom in matters of love. Our marriages aren't arranged, we get to pick a spouse based on attraction, not their dowry. We marry who we want and for better or worse, leave when we want, for our own reasons. A confession of Liza's sort by a wife in some fundamentalist Islamic cultures could set an enraged husband into a tirade of insidious violence.

In Pakistan, a woman named Zahida Perveen recently had her eyes gouged out and nose and earlobes cut off with a razor blade by her husband, who suspected, didn't even know for sure, that she was having an affair. Perveen, who was three months pregnant at the time of the attack, spoke of her ordeal to *Washington Post* reporter Pamela Constable for a story that ran on the cover of the newspaper on Monday, May 8, 2000.

"He came home from the mosque and accused me of having a bad character," said the thirty-two-year-old Perveen. "I told him it was not true, but he didn't believe me. He caught me and tied me up, and then he started cutting my face. He never said a word except, 'This is your last night.'"

While Perveen's case is extreme, reporter Constable found that this experience is not a rarity, that incidents such as these are broadly known as "honor crimes" throughout

Pakistan, and other Middle Eastern countries. As Constable writes: "Thousands of Pakistani women and girls are stabbed, burned, or maimed every year by husbands, fathers, or brothers, who believe they have brought them dishonor by being unfaithful . . ."

However civilized we like to think of ourselves, there are still some wicked crimes of passion committed every day in America, by both sexes, in all classes, in the name of jealousy and revenge. We have seen the matronly head of a prestigious East Coast private school murder her straying lover, a famous diet doctor. We have seen a young woman lop off her husband's penis with a knife, then toss it on the side of a road. We read about dumped lovers stabbing and shooting on the back streets of big cities and small towns. Yet, middle-class America has never been a culture that routinely punishes adultery with physical torture. In fact, most of the time we don't even get divorced because of it.

When a spouse comes clean about a fling, or gets caught cheating, we are more apt to turn to therapists or online advisors, such as DearPeggy.com, written by Peggy Vaughan, a woman who has been hurt, but ultimately strengthened, by infidelity. After her husband confessed he had been serially unfaithful twenty-five years ago, Peggy worked with James to reconstruct their marriage, and she went on to devote her life's work to helping others heal from affairs.

Vaughan and others have pioneered the growing movement to work through affairs, not run from them. No one likes it, and we tremble at the prospect of being deceived ourselves, but we are in childish denial if we don't accept that extramarital sex is a real possibility in the unfolding fabric of a long relationship, where both partners work and meet interesting people every day. God decreed, "Thou shalt not commit adultery," but more than half of the people who get married do. And when the deed is discovered, husbands and wives must make their own choices, based on their individual level of tolerance for anger and pain and what it could mean for their bank accounts.

Liza defected from nearly two decades of marriage to be with someone else, a choice she determined was neither right nor wrong, but one that suited her, based on emotional and financial needs. She knew her choice would have consequences, good and bad, that would ripple her life forevermore. We all know stories about marriages breaking up that cause us to cast harsh judgment: How could a mother walk out of a life with the father of her five children because she isn't in love with him anymore? How can a forty-eight-year-old man leave his wife for his twenty-six-year-old secretary? But I reiterate something stated earlier: No one knows what's going on in a marriage except the two people themselves. Although we may have strong opinions, it's a choice that can only be figured out by the person making it. We might be surprised by what our own choice would be in similar circumstances, what fork in the road we would take.

Peggy Vaughan's column at DearPeggy.com focuses on healing after affairs and draws some 70,000 readers each month. Many husbands and wives tell Vaughan that not only did she save their marriage, but quite possibly she helped save their lives. Over the past twenty years, Vaughan has built a reputation as the leading authority on recovering from affairs, drawn from her own experience with her husband's affairs early on in their marriage. She has written several books on the subject, including *The Monogamy Myth*, and coordinates a national support group, Beyond Affairs Network (BAN). She is also the expert on affairs for AOL's AskPeggy.com.

I met Vaughan in June of 1999 at a conference on marriage sponsored by the Smart Marriages organization and was struck by her natural beauty, the softness in her eyes, and the vulnerability she shows not with shame but with pride. As affairs are now outed as a real part of many marriages, this has helped Vaughan's efforts in helping couples deal frankly and responsibly with the subject, so that reconstruction can begin.

Yet, back in 1980, when James and Peggy Vaughan appeared on *Donahue*, it was unheard of for a couple to publicly discuss the fact that there had been an extramarital affair, that they had worked through it and had stayed together. Affairs were shoved under the rug and partners cried alone into their pillows, as Vaughan herself did in the late 1960s.

The Vaughans, who have been married for forty-five years, grew up together in a small town in Mississippi. The hormone-inflamed teenagers "made love on most of the back roads of Monroe County," as James recalls in the book they cowrote in 1980, *Beyond Affairs*. After a lifetime of intimacy—first friendship, then more—it was not difficult for Peggy to detect a shift in James's behavior during the start of their marriage, a shift she believed meant he was being unfaithful, which he was. As she writes in *Beyond Affairs*, "I could sense the invisible boundary he had set up to keep me at a distance—and I could only guess as to why. I didn't know he was having an affair, but I had a kind of sinking feeling that something bad was happening."

Vaughan was hesitant to grant me an interview because she feels, correctly, that the media's tendency is to sensationalize affairs, focusing on "titillation and voyeurism," rather than attempting to provide insights into the awful toll they take on marriage. I told her I wouldn't spin her words, I'd just let her talk:

We have known each other our whole lives, and in high school we started going steady. In hindsight, I see that we never made the conscious decision to get married, we just assumed we would get married. But like most of the women of my generation, I didn't even know we had a choice.

I could have been Betty Friedan's role model. When that book came out, my husband was working and I was a full-time stay-at-home mom, with one child and one on the way, and I had bought into the assumption that this was how my life was supposed to be. I had been voted the most popular, best dressed, the beauty queen of my high school, yet I never had a really strong self-image. I was raised as a strict Southern Baptist in a very religious environment. James liked my role as the dutiful wife. I was a gourmet cook. I prepared the income taxes. I packed for all his trips he made as a psychologist working at a university, and he just loved it.

Because I depended totally on him for approval, he started to pull away and think of me not as an individual, but as a stereotypical wife. Seven years before I actually found out, I suspected that James was having an affair, and it scared me to death to think that my world might not be what I thought it was, that the fairy tale was not only over, that it never existed. I even briefly contemplated suicide, but then I determined that what I really needed to do was to get stronger in order to face this crisis.

It was 1966, and I thought that I might wind up getting a divorce, and if that happened, I knew I had to continue to get stronger before I confronted him. So I didn't even let him know I was the least bit suspicious. For seven years, I kept my feelings strictly to myself, and kept working on ways to grow and feel good about myself. I started to realize that staying in a marriage needs to be something you choose to do, not something you have to do.

I was getting my own mind working, reading everything in sight, becoming involved in serious causes, including the debate about Vietnam and the growing women's movement, and attending all kinds of self-help seminars. Up to that point, I had always assumed that James was smarter than me; he was the one with the Ph.D. I began to realize that I, too, was bright, and the process of learning new things translated into tremendous personal growth, and a growing self-esteem.

Yet, during this period, in the 1960s, there was no one to talk to about affairs. I was completely isolated, ashamed and embarrassed to share anything about it. So I didn't tell a single person. Not only did I hide my suspicions and concerns, I put on this big, happy front. Nobody knew for the seven years that I was literally dying inside. And here my husband would be traveling all over the country with his job, and to Rio, and to Switzerland, and I'd be telling people, "Oh, don't you worry about James, I don't. Oh no, I trust him completely." I even had him fooled that I didn't suspect anything.

Then when he told me that yes, he'd had many affairs over the past seven years, in a way, I felt a tremendous relief. I knew the truth. I wasn't crazy; I had been right about all my suspicions from the beginning. The initial sense of relief at finally knowing was soon replaced by other questions. I thought, What's wrong with me? and What's wrong with him? But I have come to know over the years that no one is immune from affairs, and they are more prevalent than most people know, or want to believe. One of the factors that drew James into affairs was pure excitement, a curiosity for the new, a feeling that he was missing out on something. This is not to excuse it, but it helps to talk about and understand the factors that makes a partner enter into an affair. James had never had sex with anybody but me, and although we went into our marriage with the same beliefs about monogamy, after we had been married for a while, his thinking gradually changed.

This whole idea that you marry the right person and you're home free is ridiculous; what people need to understand is that this issue is never really settled, unless you have a lobotomy. The urge to have an affair may come up again and again, and that's why it is important for the couple to have a commitment to complete honesty, and from that can come a commitment to monogamy.

The trump card is a commitment to honesty in your marriage rather than being deceptive and secretive. If you commit to honesty, about being attracted to other people, and the temptation to sleep with someone else, then you are not allowing the fantasy to grow until it gets out of hand.

You can say to each other, "Let's be realistic. We know we're going to be attracted to other people. Let's make this joint commitment to be honest, to talk about our attractions, our jealousies, on an ongoing basis." That diffuses the power of acting on it, and there's no sneaking around if you can talk about it. Most people talk about affairs once they've been discovered having them. Up to that point, they block it, they believe it will never be a problem. Talking about the attraction tends to break the fantasy connection a person may have with someone else; it's no longer their own private secret.

For us, our crises have only deepened the connection. Over the years, I had breast cancer, James had prostate cancer, we had a major financial crash, and we have often felt like two people who are shipwrecked together. Today, forty-five years later, we are bound in a way that no differences and no problems can break apart. Our relationship is on a spiritual level that goes beyond husband and wife; in our togetherness, there is a universe of oneness.

Marriage, forty-five years into it, is not only this plateau; it's a steady rise and fall. I still get sad. There are times when I get depressed, absolutely. There is no such thing in a marriage that you hit this plateau and stay there. You can't know high without knowing low. It's like in a tide there is no regular pattern. People ask me if I trust my husband now; and I do trust him because I know that his intentions are good.

But no matter how great a marriage, especially women, we need to accept the fact that ultimately each of us is responsible for *ourselves, and our own happiness. You can make a tremendous difference in the degree of long-term satisfaction by making sure you don't surrender yourself. You must continue to learn and continue to become interested in new things, to be interesting. That's part of the attraction; that your spouse still doesn't know everything about you.*

Yet, anyone, anywhere is vulnerable to an affair. You can be a secluded person out in the country. It happens so fast.

In a secluded farmtown two hours from Washington, D.C., May, forty-nine, was blindsided when she discovered her husband's affair. She had what she considered "a great, sexy marriage" and a tranquil life. May is black-haired and tanned to the russet shade in a Crayola box, and we are talking on her porch overlooking cornfields. She is drinking white wine and reminiscing about her husband's affair with a "trashy bimbo" that went on for two years. The mother of two sons in college, she is still with their father, "the love of my life."

It's been a twisted and painful journey to this point of light, where she is now solidly married to a remorseful husband who has come around big time since she basically gave him his choice: Shape up, or you lose me. Like Peggy Vaughan suggests, May's willingness to hear everything about the Other Woman—her husband's reasons for straying, even what sex was like—got her to another level in marriage, "where nothing can shake us now."

Throughout much of the interview, May dabs tears from coal-colored eyes with a powder-blue Kleenex as she talks about the shock and hurt her husband's affair created for this close-knit family, considered to be wholesome and exemplary in the 4-H Club-pocked county. Her husband is the town veterinarian, May is a homemaker, their boys are smart and athletic and nice. Here is the nightmare they all endured while the town's beloved vet had a midlife crisis:

We met in college and we've been married for twenty-six years. I fell for him right away; he's just a very masculine man, and we both like to sail. He was studying to be a vet, and I was working as a nurse. He was everything to me, absolutely. And it continued like that for our entire marriage. I always thought we were happier than any couple I knew. That's why this affair just nearly killed me; it came out of nowhere. I absolutely never, ever suspected. It happened three years ago, and went on for quite a while.

After I found out, he asked me if I knew something was going on. And I said no, that I was a fool. And he said, "You're not a fool, you just had faith in me," and that made him feel really bad. Later, he said it happened because he wasn't doing that well at the clinic, and he was working harder and harder and making less money. The money thing is hard for the male ego. This other lady must have been an escape from all that. And we were in with this group of people who were doing really well. And he just started feeling inferior, that's not an excuse but that's what happened. And this other lady was there and she was uneducated and made him feel real important. She was a divorcee with five children.

And it wasn't like she was some young thing; she's our age. I knew her, she was one of his regular clients, she had dogs, and it was always obvious that she had this big crush on him. I never even suspected one thing for a long, long time. We were having a wonderful sexual relationship. And then suddenly, it got to a point where he was very quiet. And sex stopped. I asked him what was wrong, and he would tell me he was upset about work. And it made me so depressed I started drinking too much because I was so lonely.

One night I heard a lot of yelling in my living room. One of my sons was yelling at his father, because he had found out about the affair. Turns out the boys would hear him go downstairs at night after I went to sleep and talk to this lady on the telephone.

I'd be asleep, and sometimes I would hear the phone ring three times but never thought about it. But that was their signal for him to call. The first thing I said was, "Did you have sex with her?" And he said he didn't. For a week or so I believed that they just had this friendship, but then all of a sudden everything came out.

I was just so trusting. I grew up with this man, and never imagined he could cheat on me. When I found out, the first thing I wanted was just for us to go back to our normal life. I told him I'd take him back. I wanted our family to be just like it had been. It was like I was in denial. But I told him to tell her good-bye and just come back home. And we tried that for a while, but I could tell he'd come home real quiet and that he was still seeing her. Turns out the kids were doing all sorts of things behind my back; they were in such pain about this, also. They were sending her letters telling her she was evil and that she better not come near their father again or her life was in danger. They actually confronted her in person once, following their father's car to her house. I'm happy no one got hurt that night.

Then one morning my husband said to me that he wasn't sure he could live in our house anymore, that he felt like he had to explore this new person, that he had feelings for her. It was terrible, but we separated. God, the children were so mad at their dad. They would tell him that he could never love anyone else like he loved their mom.

This woman had a chain-link fence, shag carpet, a big, mean dog. One night, my husband came back over here, and he must have been struck by how different our house is, clean, soft music, good food, his children around. And he started complaining to me about his lady friend, how stupid she was about things, how unhappy he was, and I just looked at him and said, "Ya know, I don't give a shit about her, and I don't give a shit what you do. Don't you dare talk to me about her." Another time he came over and we had a really long talk and he told me how bitter he was about some of our friends with their big houses and big vacations, people who didn't work nearly as hard as he worked. Then he asked me if I had an affair, because there was a point in our marriage that I guess he thought I did. I told him I would never have an affair, that I had always been in love with him.

Then, I asked him, "Are you in love with her?" And he said, "Yes." I said, "Get the hell out of here right now, forever." The next day he came back for all of his clothes. And I drank and drank and drank that whole week, I was just numbing myself. I couldn't eat anything. I got very skinny. He tried to come over again that week and I wouldn't even let him in; I just told him not to call me anymore unless he had a business matter to discuss. And he said to me, "You can't be happy without me." I just looked at him, and at this point, I don't know why, but I felt really strong and said back: "You just watch how happy I can be without you. All this pain you've caused me, I'm going to be real happy without you around anymore." And he was just shocked, but it felt real good for me, it was something I should have told him months ago.

And you know what happened? I started to get strong without him. I realized that I could live without him. I stopped drinking so much, and started going out with my women friends, and gained some weight, and just hung out with my sons. They were so good to their mother during this time, really protective of me.

One night, when I wasn't home, my husband called and talked to my oldest son. And he told me how he said, "I love your mom so much and I have made such a mess of everything and I want to be with her. I want to make love to her. I want to spend the rest of my life with her. And I don't know what to do. I've destroyed everything." That's a lot to heap onto a kid, but my son and I talked and we cried and cried.

The next day I called my husband and said, "Let's meet somewhere for coffee." Then I asked him to tell me everything *that I didn't have the guts to ask him about all these months. How long was this thing going on? Where did she work? What was sex like? And we just hashed things out. He said that he couldn't stand living at her house anymore. That he had tried to redo her house so it would look more like our house. And he said he would try and make them nice dinners, light candles and play music, like we did, but that it wasn't the same. That it was just horrible and made him miss us even more.*

I realized then that I still loved him, and always loved him. And that I would take him back, even after everything he did. One morning I went out grocery shopping and came back home and his Oldsmobile was in the driveway, and there he was, lying on top of our bed. And he said, "I know I don't deserve to be here, but I want to move back home." I said to him, "If you come back, you can have no communication with that lady." I told him that he must tell me if she tries to see him or calls him, that this time he has to tell me everything.

And I said if I find out there has been any contact at all, that he is gone for good, forever. And that was it between them, he told her he wanted to be back with his wife and children. Our marriage is stronger than ever before; it's like if we made it through this nightmare nothing can shake us now.

But it did happen, and I haven't wiped it out completely; how can you? It's always down there somewhere. But I do forgive him. What are my choices? To not be with the man I love for the rest of my life, someone I know loves me and loves the kids? He is my husband, and he has done everything he can to atone for what he has done, other than stab himself in the heart.

May's story of financial strains driving her husband into an affair reminds me of something my father used to tell me when I was entering the job market at the advent of feminism in the middle 1970s. Women were making unprecedented strides and salaries in fields previously dominated by men, in medicine, business, and law. My dad would say that no matter how high women rose in their professions, his admittedly archaic view of marriage was that the husband should be the more successful of the two, that most male egos couldn't take an unequal balance of economic power.

He once told me he also found that it was easier for a man to be friends with other men who made about as much money as he did, that males are competitive in that way. Although his view is politically incorrect and comes from a different era, I think he was generally right about men and money. Income is more a yardstick of success and power among men than women; women compete on other playing fields, often measuring success by who has the most physical beauty or the most emotional fulfillment.

Finances were not a problem for Jacob, a strikingly handsome journalist from Sarasota. The choice about which direction his marriage was headed was made by his wife of eighteen years, when she told him she was in love with someone else, a woman in her twenties. A competitive bicyclist who recently celebrated his forty-eighth birthday, Jacob moved through many stages as his wife grappled with her sexual identity, from rage to devastation to "I've gotta get her back." The couple worked hard in therapy to reconstruct their marriage, but his wife ended up getting clear that she prefers women to men, and she moved out of their house. Their two daughters now live primarily with Jacob. Here is his side of the story:

When I first found out and I told my closest guy friends she was a lesbian, they would say, "Have you put her stuff out on the street yet? How can you stand to stay with this woman?" But that was not a problem for me. I was totally committed to this relationship for a good eight months after I discovered the betrayal. I believe in marriage. I took my marriage vows seriously, and I intended to keep them. And when it became apparent that the marriage was over, I was very sad that I was not going to be able to do what I said I would do at my wedding.

I know a lot of happy marriages, and I think we had one for many years. Happy marriages happen with people who are content within themselves and not searching for something in somebody else. These are people who are intellectually alive but their intellectual pursuits are within the boundaries of marriage, these are people who like to do things together, they like to go out on dates. I mean, we got to the point in the last two years of our marriage where I had to ask my wife for a date three weeks in advance, and she'd be like, "Well, I don't know if we can afford to," or "We were just out and I don't want to be away from the girls." After a while I realized these were excuses because my wife didn't want to go out with me, and it was a problem, because I could never just be spontaneous.

It wasn't easy for her to fall in love with a woman. I used to find her crying in the basement. I'd hug her and say, "That's okay, we'll get over this." I wanted her to get through whatever she had to get through so she would come back to me and our family could be whole again. I'm no saint. Would I have liked to pummel her? Did I imagine sending a hit man over? Hell, yeah. My wife and I had a very good sexual relationship. We gave each other great pleasure, and it was shocking to find out that she didn't like having sex with a man.

When we first met, it wasn't love at first sight. This was a gradual falling in love, and throughout our marriage we would fall romantically in and out of love. But the marriage was lonely, and it is excruciating to expect warmth and companionship from your spouse and instead end up feeling intense loneliness.

I saw what we lacked in our relationship and I was willing to work on it once things started to unravel. I was totally open to doing anything to save my family. I loved being a family, even if our marriage lacked some very fundamental aspects, like human warmth. Every human being needs to be touched and to hug and if they don't, that drains away a lot of relationships. You see these bumper stickers, "Have you hugged your child today?" The sticker should say: "Have you hugged your spouse today?"

I am a naturally cuddly person, a hugger, but my wife is not. And that really wounded me in my relationship. I would ask for it, to hug, and she would say to me, "If you ask for it you won't get it." And after fifteen years of this, I came to an understanding that this is not going to be the greatest love story of all time. But I was satisfied with what I did have, a long-term relationship built on a solid foundation of love and children and of making a home together. I was committed to my marriage lasting forever, totally. I was loyal to this woman with my body, with my heart, with my soul, with my mind.

I mean, that's who I am. My mom and dad were married for over fifty years and with that as a foundation, those were my expectations and that was my goal. And I think one of the reasons I am suffering so much now is not that I miss this particular woman but that I miss being married and being a family. I hate signing forms now when you apply for credit cards and having to check in the category marked S, for separated. I always loved checking the M, for married.

I accepted the betrayal. I accepted that she may have a thing for women. I figured that I would absorb that blow because I adore being married and because I adore my family. For a while there I went into a high school mode of wooing her with flowers, champagne, candles, weekends away. But I eventually found out that even though my wife said, "Yes, let's try," she had already checked out. We would go away for a weekend and I'd be thinking we were having a beautiful time and I'd get back and would see in her emails that she was longing for someone else.

This whole thing has devastated me but, funny, it also has given me an intense resolve to get into a lasting relationship again. I know now that even though I was committed to reestablishing the marriage, and fought like hell for it, it was out of my control. She absolved me, in a sense, by saying that there was nothing I could have done about her sexuality. You know, it's easier for me to have been left for a woman than for a man. My poker buddies would ask me the same question, and I'm pretty clear about it. It's easier for me because my wife has chosen a woman. Much easier. Why is that? I can't compete. I don't have the equipment.

I'm a very male man, although I do come with a strong feminine side, who is sensitive and needs to nurture and be nurtured. All the things that we ascribe to the feminine, I have as well, but I'm also extremely male at the same time, very testosterone heavy, very aggressive, and during this whole thing, very hostile. It's been real hard on our girls. The oldest one is thirteen, and she's got some deep pain about this. There is anger at her mother and fear that she's going to grow up to be a lesbian, too, that it's inherited. The best thing I can do is just shut up and listen, and she is very bright and in touch with her feelings and can articulate them, so she's not holding everything in, and that's good. These girls love their mother, they should. She is a good mother. But the oldest one is furious at her. She tells me that a lot and I just say, "Well, that's okay for now, and I'm sure it will ease up over time," and it has.

What I have learned from this mess is that next time I have a relationship, I'm going to look for a depth, a comfort level, we did not have. My brother said it best. When he was beginning his relationship with the woman who turned out to be his wife, he knew right away she was the right one. I asked, "Why did you choose her?" And he said when he was with her, "I felt like I was home." They've been married for twenty-eight years.

I will look for that next time. I will look for physical comfort that is not just sex, a human connection. There's a level of pain I've endured I never want to go through again. As for the children, I am trying to ease them into dealing with having a lesbian mother. There are a lot of struggles in our culture for homosexu-

als. I am also making sure they have a lot of strong, female, heterosexual role models. I am teaching them that you come into a relationship as a whole being, and when you do and are not looking for wholeness somewhere else, you are in a position of really giving love and receiving love.

I love Jacob's recollection of how his brother felt when he met his wife, "like I was home," because it validates what I first felt about Chuck. In my gut, I knew I was home, that I could be myself, that I didn't have to impress him, that he didn't make me nervous. I polished off a huge plate of sushi on our first date, I'm talking gobs of raw fish, then drank a couple Kirin beers straight from the bottle. Chuck watched me and smiled.

Years later, he told me the reason he was staring so intently was not because he was enchanted, but because there was a piece of yellow sea urchin clinging to my cheek.

We all remember guys we have dated who put butterflies in our stomach, who set us on edge, who we'd go to dinner with and couldn't even get one morsel down. I used to mistake that for true love, you know, convince myself I was being hit with the thunderbolt real thing. During these sick romances, my sister, Fran, would quickly reel me back to earth. She would meet this man of the moment I was mad about, then call me later that night with this kiss-off review: "You are not yourself around him. Forget him; it's not going anywhere."

When Fran saw Chuck and I together, from the get-go, it was thumbs up: "You are definitely on the same wavelength," was her initial response. "You even look alike." And she was right. With Chuck, I am home—in my head, in my heart, in my sexuality. Beyond friendship and compatibility, we all need some degree of ongoing crackle for a marriage to make it. Having sex every six months, or once a year, as some couples do, is not enough. It is a direct route to trouble.

Kate has the friendship component, but not the crackle. She is forty-seven, Rubenesque, and has straight brown bangs and hair that hangs to the middle of her back. She and her husband live on the East Coast and have no children. When she is not working her primary job as a hair stylist, she also plays various string instruments in pickup bands. I met her on a photo shoot, during which she overheard me talking about the book I was writing on marriage. She pulled me aside and whispered: "I have a story for you."

Like Jacob, she, too, feels a lack of intimacy in her marriage. But at least he had sex; she has nearly none. This past summer, at a music camp in Oregon, Kate met a man she believes she loves. She was bursting to talk about him, no longer able to keep to herself the "elation and confusion." In nearly two decades of marriage she had never strayed, but she was about to. Her fantasy man from the West was coming East on business, and they were planning a rendezvous. Here is how she expresses her mixed emotions, about a marriage she is resigned to stay in, and about a man who makes her want to run away.

He was in my fiddle class at music camp. Immediately, he introduced himself, and then he started to sit next to me. And I thought, Okay, this is all right. One night, I was playing in a dance band and he comes up and taps me on the elbow and asks me if I want to waltz. I love to dance and never get to. My husband is not much of a dancer. So I was thrilled to dance, I studied dance for many years, and I can dance pretty well. He was very deft, very good at leading, and that was the moment that I felt it, the magic.

Over the next few nights we had a couple more dances, and this led up to a big costume party. We had to dress as a tune. I picked "Squirrel in a Tree," and I decided to be very alluring. I washed my hair and let it dry naturally and it was everywhere.

Then I stuck branches in it and green leaves, because I was supposed to be a tree. I really wanted to look beautiful. That night, he pulled me out on the dance floor and we had a blast. I could feel myself radiating, oozing; I couldn't help it, I was starting to come alive.

I took long walks after that alone in the woods because I was very upset with myself for feeling that way. I am married! But I was just so drawn to this man. The last day of camp I was waiting on a log in the sun for my bus to take me to the airport. He walked over and said, "Well, how about a hug?" I didn't know what to do. Then he said, "Oh, come on, it's not going to hurt you to hug me." So I gave him a little nothing of a hug.

Then I thought: This is bullshit. I'm going to be honest with this man. I patted the log and said, "Sit down. I need to talk to you." I told him I had a crush on him, and I'd been walking around feeling like an adolescent and I've been married for eighteen years. And he said that he was married, too, and had three daughters, the oldest was nineteen. Then I slapped him on the arm and said, "Oh good, you are married also. Then nothing can happen between us."

· But then he said that he had been experiencing the same pull. And I said I was glad it wasn't just me. I had thought maybe my hormones were going crazy. He asked again for a hug. I said, "Well, okay." So we hugged for a long time, it felt wonderful. My whole torso was just broiling with sensation. Throughout that whole week I felt like I was falling in love with him, but I didn't admit it to myself until that moment, and after he left it was a terrible and teary revelation. I hadn't felt like this for a long, long time.

My husband met me when I was on the rebound from an incredible love that destroyed me, and killed any of these sensations for good, or so I thought. I was totally in love with someone when I was twenty. He was twenty-three, and he ended up breaking up with me after a year. This was a young man I wanted to spend the rest of my life with. I have not felt that same irresistible attraction, that absolute chemistry, since then, certainly not with my husband, until I met this other man.

A couple weeks ago my camp friend called because he was coming on a business trip out East, and he said: "Maybe we can go dancing," and I told him that I'd love to. When I heard that voice I had the most visceral reaction, you can't even imagine. The irony is that afternoon before he called I had been thinking about him, and fell asleep and dreamt about him and had an orgasm. Then he woke me up with his phone call.

Yet, I know in my heart there is a sense of doom to our relationship, like the Titanic. I am married, he is married, he has children. But I am still receptive to something new happening. I've been married for eighteen years to a very nice man who I am not passionate about. I was never attracted to him in that way, but by the time I met him, I had gone through several passionate relationships that had gone very badly. When I was with my husband, I always felt good about myself. He is reliable and faithful, he cherishes me. But there is no passion.

What keeps me going is that I know, even with that flaw, our marriage is probably still better than 99 percent of the marriages out there. I don't let myself get depressed that we only have sex once every two months. We tried for several years to have children, but there were fertility problems. When I hit forty-one, I said, "Let's stop trying. I can't do this anymore." That was a hard thing for both of us to go through, physically and emotionally. But over the years we have built up a lot of love and mutual respect. There has not been a lot of sexual excitement, and all of a sudden I miss that because of what I felt last summer when I met this other man.

Of course, I really don't know him at all. It was pure fantasy, until we finally did get to spend a Saturday together when he came to town in March. We drove to a beautiful park, got out of the car and he hugged me and kissed me. Then we stopped about every few yards and hugged and kissed and groped and laid down under the sun and talked and groped some more. After a long walk along the river, we stopped at a tiny, dark French bistro to have lunch. Then we checked into a hotel, went to a room and pulled out our violins and played for about forty-five minutes.

We laid down on the bed and kissed some more, did a little heavy petting, and then he decided it wasn't a good idea to have sex. He said, "Let's have dinner instead." This whole day I had a bad nervous stomach. But we went down to the hotel restaurant and split a club sandwich and a green salad and a beer. Then we went back upstairs, ostensibly to get my coat and my fiddle, and ended up kissing and groping again.

At this point, I really wanted to just do it. So I removed my shirt and my bra. I was purposely trying to work him up, and he just loved it. He ended up taking his pants off and sitting on the edge of the bed, so there we were, I was naked from the waist up and he was naked from the waist down. And I was sort of holding him down there, and we were kissing, and we were on the brink of more, then he said, "No please, I don't want to hurt you. You need to go home to your husband knowing that you didn't sleep with someone else." So I stepped back, put my clothes on, he walked me down to the car, we said good-bye, and he went back to his hotel.

I spent that evening and the next day flying high as a kite, wanting nothing more than to see him again and make love all over the place. Monday morning I had a meditation class and a session with my therapist, and between the two I realized it was probably a hopeless situation. The reality is he's not free. He's not particularly happy in his marriage, and while he has had other affairs, he's not going to leave his wife of twenty-five years or his family. The reality is that I am married, too, in a passionless marriage with no children, but I don't want to hurt my husband. He is a good man.

But, you know, I haven't seen another man naked other than my husband in more than twenty years, and it felt wonderful. And this man could be the love of my life, but he's not available and I'm not going to screw around on my husband—at least I don't think I'm going to screw around on my husband. Lately I've been thinking I definitely want to see this man again, that I just may have to go visit my cousin in Oregon.

The destructive, yet exalting, madness of lust is what leads many marrieds astray. Yet, naughty romances that can initially appear to be divinely inspired often end up feeling like earthly disasters. I heard from many spouses who succumbed to temptation, more than Kate's tease of a petting session for one afternoon. We're talking about going all the way, for months, or years. Here is a contemporary extramarital affair, as recounted by Beatrice, from Texas. This thirty-five-year-old waitress is wiry and tough and the mother of two young children. Her lover drove her to drink and to drugs and nearly to divorce. During our conversations, she usually sounded out of control.

Some days she'd be panting, so in love, exuberant about finding an escape from her "marriage without a soul." Other times, she'd be sobbing because her lover could not see her that week; he was away on one of his frequent overseas trips or had family obligations, like planning his wife's surprise party. After interviewing many people who have been in affairs, the evolution of this one seems generic. First, a wonderful lunch. Next, necking in cars. Then, a hotel rendezvous, followed by lots of other trysts, then feeling awful about sneaking around. Here is Beatrice's account of a hard collision between fantasy and reality that occurred when she discovered that the true Mr. Right was the husband she married six years ago.

I knew what I was getting into when I got involved with a guy I had a bad crush on in high school. I always felt a strong attraction to him, but then he started going steady with a friend of mine and that was that. He went to college down state and then moved to California, and got married out there. Then I got married and really didn't think about him at all, especially when I starting having babies. Marriage, right from the get-go, was hard for me. My husband and I fought constantly or didn't talk at all, sort of like what I saw in my own parents' broken marriage.

Then when my husband and I had kids, we would give them all our attention and be so tired it was like there was nothing more to give. With two babies, an affair was the furthest thing from my mind. But I did notice that when I would be working my shift at the restaurant and single men would be seated in my station, I could be a real flirt. One day, who comes in the restaurant? The boy from high school who is now a tall, handsome man. Hadn't seen him for years.

We talked for a while, about our kids and our jobs. He said, "You are still so pretty." I was ecstatic. My husband never told me I was pretty. The next day I did something stupid: I called him at work and asked him to have lunch.

We went to a Mexican restaurant and had a real good time, talking and laughing mostly about people we knew as kids. We were still talking when we walked to our cars, and he kissed me good-bye. Now, no man had kissed me like that except my husband. He stuck his tongue so deep in my mouth.

Two days passed, three days, and I couldn't stand it, so I called him. Made it sound really casual but asked him to have lunch again. That lunch went on for two hours and I heard everything about his marriage. He said that he and his wife had really separate lives. I told him the same thing was going on with me. We ended up complaining about how bad our spouses were, and then laughed about how maybe we should have ended up together.

My husband is a decent man and he makes a good living, but in the excitement category, he doesn't score really high. And this other man was real rich and real exciting. We began having lunch two times a week, and we were becoming real close. I would get a neighbor to watch my babies and go out, dressed in some killer outfit. After a couple months, instead of kissing good-bye, we'd get into a car and really go at it.

One afternoon, instead of lunch, we rented a motel room, a real dive. And we had sex on a twin bed; I remember the bedspread was this ugly flowered thing that smelled like cigarettes. It was so strange, I don't even remember it. It was like my mind and body separated. But even with the sex being weird, being with a man who wanted to talk and hear about my problems made me feel good. But when I'd get home, I'd feel real scummy. Here's Mommy, just screwed another man, fixing dinner, waiting for her husband.

By this point, my lover was talking about leaving his wife to be with me. I would play along and it would get me excited but it was like something I couldn't really imagine doing. Like, Oh, sure, I'm gonna leave these babies? Tell you the truth, I don't know what I was doing. I see now I was copying my own parents' bad marriage where they'd either be yelling at each other or ignoring each other. I knew they both had lovers they were escaping to. After fifteen years together, they finally split.

Here's the weird thing, though. I always liked sex with my husband, even when we were at our lowest points. It's like an animal attraction. With this other man, I was never swept away. I should have ended it so many times realizing what I did, but the longer things went on he became a fix I needed. I was hooked on love, a sick love. I was an addict.

When he didn't call for even one day I would get real depressed and take Valium or drink a bottle of wine. And the really *awful part of being in love with someone married is that you can't just call them or drop into their kitchen for coffee. You are always sneaking and lying, and God, your spouse really pays the penalty. I was just a bitch to him during this time, not to mention how distracted I must have been with those kids.*

Well, there are many morals to this story. A cheating man is a cheating man, and if he's cheating on his wife, he's probably cheating on you, too. Listen to your heart. Being a cheating wife felt slimy and wrong to me, it was killing me. I felt like I was going against God. In church on Sundays, I would feel like my higher self and my lower self were in a war, sorta like the angel versus the devil.

The end came by itself. One morning we were having sex on the couch in his friend's apartment where we used to meet and I looked up at him and he just looked real sorry to me. I saw the real naked guy, not the prince. His white belly was showing, and his khaki pants and boxers were crumpled at his feet. Right there, I knew it was over. I was turned off, and I could tell he was turned off, too. I'd seen my husband exactly like that lots of times, his jeans rolled around his shoes when we'd make love for a quickie, and the times I saw my husband like that it was always a turn-on. With all our fighting and carrying on, I am always real hot for my husband.

Well, now there's a permanent black mark on me, and it is a dirty secret I will carry to my grave. My husband would just shoot me if he knew. I wish this guy and I could have just kissed and left it at that. Because I knew in the end I'd never run off with him and split my family. After much plowing around inside myself, I see that I set out to destroy my marriage because I just believed that marriage isn't forever and once you have problems with one husband, you just pack up and move on to the next guy. Watching my parents leave each other and just break each other's hearts, I was afraid to get real close to a man.

In an affair, you are playing it safe. You're not close to your husband and you can't get real close to someone else's husband, either.

Today, I'm trying to work out the problems I have with my husband. I've been a lot nicer to him, and I make sure I flatter him. And I've asked him to pay more attention to me. I told him I need that. We're having more fun, and I'm not looking for some white knight to take me away. My husband may not be the life of the party, but he is my husband. I pray real hard for forgiveness, but I will never forgive myself. I'm just glad I woke up before I ruined everything.

There are several hard truths to take away from Beatrice's story. Marriage is a sacred covenant that needs to be valued, not devalued. Illicit love can never really be satisfying. And, finally, if we do fall down, it is possible to pick ourselves back up.

For the past twenty-five years, attorney Robert Liotta has been listening to husbands and wives complain that they are not getting enough love from their partners. He has heard lots of stories like these, but unlike Beatrice and Kate, the people telling the stories are in his office because they can't stand it anymore, and they want out. Liotta has watched his profession go from a point where divorce was uncommon and granted generally only for grounds of adultery or cruelty to the no-fault divorce in which anyone can split for nearly any reason, large or small.

Liotta has handled some of Washington's most illustrious splits in the circles of media and politics, including Nora Ephron and Carl Bernstein and the divorce of Tony Rodham, Senator Hillary Clinton's brother, who was married to Nicole Boxer, Senator Barbara Boxer's daughter. He was also the lawyer for a landmark Maryland case, in which he successfully represented a lesbian mother, who conceived her child with artificial insemination, against claims of custody and visitation rights filed by her former live-in lover.

Married for seventeen years to artist Barbara Josephs Liotta, he is the father of two sons, ages thirteen and fifteen. Being immersed in decaying marriages every working day has given him incentive and inspiration to pay keen attention to the health of his own relationship. As he says: "I listen to my clients and try never to make those same mistakes."

Italian-American and raised in New Jersey, he is direct and fast-talking and passionate about his work. Here is Liotta's long view of marriage, cultivated in a city where fickle romances are a way of life.

The general public thinks the main reason couples get divorced is that someone is having an affair. But in the vast majority of the cases I see, the affair itself is not the cause of the demise of the marriage. Marriages fall apart because the relationship is bad, and an affair is generally just a symptom of an otherwise distressed relationship.

I've had lots of women and men come in and say, "My marriage has been a disaster for the last five years or ten years or fifteen years, and I'm in this other relationship and that is what is catapulting me to do something about it." So, again, it's not the affair, it's the entire marriage that's been a problem.

When I first started divorce work in 1975, it was the start of the divorce revolution. And I remember being so shocked at the changing status of marriage: This woman came in, she was in her late thirties, very attractive, very well dressed, she had a business of her own. And she said cooly, "I don't like being married to this person, I have another person I like much better and I just want to get divorced." After she had gotten divorced, she called me up and she said, "I've never been so happy in my life. And I'm not getting married to this other guy. I'm just running my business and living a nice life." That was the first time I saw a woman say, "I've got my own life. I've got my own ability to take care of myself." Fortunately, there were no children.

People will often come in and say that they only have sex every six months, or once a year, and it's perfunctory; I hear that a lot. And so someone will start an affair. I am still surprised at the number of people who don't communicate. I mean, they don't talk at all. They don't even know what the other person has done in the past week. The husband might come home every night at eight o'clock and leave at eight o'clock in the morning. They don't have a clue what that person has done or who he's seen. They literally say good morning and good night and that's it.

There are very few new stories; I don't want to nod when a new person comes in here and say, "Yeah, yeah, I've heard it before," but I have. The couple doesn't talk, there is no intimacy, so there is no sex. Those are the marriage breakers. Or there might be a marriage where one person is abusive, always critical, screams a lot in front of the kids, and creates a basic horror of a living situation. When someone finally does something about it, there's a great sense of relief.

Then I see late-life divorces, people in their seventies, married fifty years. They have grandchildren. Basically what happens is that the men and women are leading separate lives, taking separate vacations, maybe someone has met someone else. They come in and say, "I've been miserable with this person for the past few decades and I've only got maybe ten more years to live so why should I be married to him or to her?"

It's the people in their twenties in new marriages that really shock me, there's no emotion. The come in and say calmly, "I'd like to get divorced." I ask why? They tell me, "Well, we've been together for a couple years and it just isn't working out. Could you just write us up an agreement?" I hear nothing about their lives, their feelings, their pain. It's all business. And, of course, there are no kids to fight about. I see this all the time. Easy in, easy out.

A newer story I hear more and more is people who come in and say that their spouse has just announced that he or she is gay and wants to leave. Before, they used to stay married and had a closeted gay life. And frankly it's the men who get more upset about it than the women. Often, it comes out of nowhere. These are people who often have reasonable sex lives with their spouses. And it raises a whole lot of issues for divorce lawyers, in terms of homosexual visitation for that person who is not a biological parent.

I make my income doing divorce law, but I am a great believer in marriage. Very often, after an hour-long interview with somebody, I'll say, "It doesn't sound to me like this marriage is irretrievable. Have you tried counseling?" Sometimes, people will tell me, "This has been going on forever and there's no hope." But I'm seeing more people open to going into therapy.

Clients range from eighteen to seventy-five, but probably my largest group is middle-age. It's the classic midlife crisis. People decide that something else is out there, or that they've missed out on life, and that a new spouse will cure their dissatisfaction. The whole AIDS epidemic really slowed down sexual promiscuity outside marriage. There used to be a sense that you could go out and have a wild life and there were no consequences. I remember cases back in the seventies when the wife would be upset because the husband had three girlfriends. I don't see very much of that now.

I also see a lot of one partner being totally shocked that the other person wants a divorce. Just blindsided, like they never saw it coming. They think everything was perfectly fine and then they hear what their spouse has really been thinking all these years. It's classic, and very sad.

The man in this particular scenario has been very busy at work, or with his friends; he doesn't spend much time talking to his wife. And the wife has been depressed and miserable at home. And she comes in here and says, "I keep trying to talk to him and he won't talk to me, he doesn't know me, he doesn't understand me, he doesn't want to understand." The husband never noticed that anything was wrong because he's been busy doing other things, or he was afraid to look at what was really going on in his relationship. I am constantly surprised at the number of people who come in and say, "I didn't know there was a problem." I mean, this person didn't know anything was wrong for fifteen and twenty years, a time frame another person has interpreted as sheer misery.

I learn a lot from my clients; I tell them, "I listen to you and try not to make the same mistakes in my own marriage." You need to take time out on a fairly regular basis to just sit down with your partner and say, "Tell me what's wrong, tell me what's right. What are your problems?" And you know, it sounds silly. But to actually sit down face-to-face and say, "We're going to have a discussion right now about us and our marriage," that is a very positive step. It may not be fun, but I have learned it is essential. It's like holding a stethoscope to the marriage.

Since the time Barbara and I were first married, we try and go to lunch every week. Or we ask each other: "You got any complaints?" We learned this other communication tool from a friend and I thought it was silly, but we tried it and it's kind of fun. You have to lie down on the living room floor with your heads away from each other, not next to each other, and just sort of look at the ceiling and say, "Okay, tell me what you're thinking about us." You each get five minutes to say what you want to say and you can't interrupt each other.

People ask me a lot, "Okay, Robert, so what does it take to stay married?" And I tell them that it comes down to this: You have to work on being intimate. That means taking time, and making time, to be together. You have to plan it. Especially if you've got kids in the house. Some of these couples getting divorced, especially some of these young ones, they never see each other. One is working in Los Angeles this week, one is in New York, and maybe in the course of a year they spend twenty nights together. And this is a disaster. There's got to be some togetherness. You have got to go out to talk, make time for sex, have fun. You have to remember why you chose this person in the first place.

I've learned this from my wife more than anybody else; you have to remember to court your spouse. It really doesn't hurt to bring home flowers every now and then. It doesn't hurt to dress up for dinner. The problems come when you feel like your life is too ordinary, that there is no excitement. You know, you've been married twenty years, your kids are almost off to college, and you feel like a robot. It's this awful sense that life is passing you by.

But because of the work that I do, I can tell you that what sits on the other side of the fence isn't any better. I know that if you cross over to be with someone else, they may have more baggage than you have. I don't see any greener grass.

No, I don't see anybody who's left their spouse and gone on to some magnificent, wonderful, perfect relationship that solved all their problems. They are still fifty years old. They still have kids. They still have an ex-spouse. How does their life change? It doesn't; you're just picking up new problems. I mean, sure, I can see someone saying, "I'm going to live in Antarctica and completely change my life." But going out and getting a new spouse? What does that do, really? You are still you.

I encourage people in a marriage that clearly can be salvaged to stay together for the children. You can scare somebody out of divorce just by telling them how much it's going to cost and how poor they're going to be for the next ten years. I say, "Oh, so you make $125,000 a year and your wife is unemployed and you've got a two-year-old, a four-year-old, and a seven-year-old and you want a divorce? Well, you know it's going to cost you $5,000 a month plus part of the mortgage and you're *going to see your kids maybe a couple times a week." They say, "Wow, that sounds horrible." And I say, "Yeah, it is horrible." Some go find another lawyer; others go back home.*

Have I seen people get divorced and remarry and be happier? Yes. Because there are some truly terrible marriages. Probably thirty-five percent of the people who come into my office really ought to be divorced. Not only are they not soul mates, they are vicious enemies who are destroying each other and destroying their kids. But more than half of the people that I see could make their marriages work. Would it take sacrifice? Yes. Would they be perfectly happy? No. But they certainly could make it if they worked at it.

I actually like it when I have to return retainer fees. Somebody gives me a few thousand dollars and I make some phone calls, write a few letters. And I don't hear from them for six months, then all of a sudden I get a call or letter saying, "Mr. Liotta, I'm sort of embarrassed. But my husband and I have decided to try it again, so could I have my money back?"

I mean, I don't like giving money back. But I'm pleased for the people. And I have plenty of other business. It never slacks off. It's just too easy today for married people to say, "I quit."

The Surrender

Loving someone at the moment they are asking for it because they need it even though you don't want to give it is the ultimate surrender in marriage.
And it takes practice, discipline, just like any other art.

I know a captivating and iconoclastic man in London, Paul Smith, the fashion designer who turned menswear on its head with his neon brights, alternative prints, and baggy, grandfatherly shapes. Still shaking up fashion after more than twenty years in the trade, Smith's read on his retro-futuristic vision, that now includes womenswear, is: "I'm very into change." Yet, he is very not into change when it comes to relationships. Smith has been with the same partner, Pauline, since 1967, a woman whose two sons he helped raise since they were babies. Theirs is a union not formalized and defined by marriage vows, but by a longstanding love which he says "allows partners to have some space." Space for Smith, who has Paul Smith boutiques internationally, means spending most of his time away from England, overseeing his distribution in Europe and in Japan.

"I see balance in a relationship as having a 'you win, I win' attitude," says Smith. "You need to understand the other person's point of view, without judgment. It means allowing your mind to calm down after a busy day, and realizing that her less busy day is still as important. Actually, Pauline and I are very different than each other in many ways."

She is a painter who thrives on working completely alone. Smith is all over, always with people, traveling seven months out of the year, often to exotic places. The last postcard I got from him was stamped Vietnam. "I think this distance is a good point that can help a relationship, the man and woman can fully develop who they are. You are giving each other that space part in which self-expression can be realized, to be theatrical, to flirt, to do business, to do all the things human beings need to do to be creative."

I asked Smith if it's all so perfect why they have never felt compelled to get married. He says, after thirty-three years together, "We have never had that conversation. Pauline and I have never discussed it, because we presumably don't think it would make any difference. It couldn't be any better, and who knows, psychologically it could be worse."

Smith's parents got married, built a house on an empty piece of land, and lived there for sixty years. With that example and his own experience in a committed relationship, his concise wisdom about making it in the long haul is not to dwell on where you've been or where you're headed, but to be fully where you are.

"I'm a very uncomplicated person," shrugs Smith. "I don't over-analyze anything, I don't clutter my head with needless thoughts. And in the case of Pauline, I've never had to think about it. It's just been there. A relationship has to be fresh, new, but the point is not to try and regain one's youth. The point is not to have lost it in the first place. How do you do that? Never over-analyze anything. And be self-disciplined enough to keep reinventing yourself.

"We all get older, but we can keep youthful in our heads. By suddenly learning a language, by realizing the joy of new experiences. I happen to be with a woman who is intelligent and has a strong will, so she is constantly learning new things. This keeps her new to me. I don't follow the obvious route, I take risks, I don't go down the secure path and I have a partner who does the same.

"Pauline keeps reinventing herself all the time; at the moment she is learning the crawl. Although she is a very good swimmer she has never been taught the crawl. She has started reading Proust, and is now on book four. We have wonderful conversations over supper; we have never lost that electricity."

I love Paul's read on the importance of reinventing yourself as a boon to sustaining a long-term partnership. New knowledge or mastery of a new sport or a reconnection with a hobby you once loved is what creates a sense of purpose in your life, and with that kick comes enhanced self-esteem. Yesterday I ran into a forty-six-year-old acquaintance, a woman who could only be called frumpy and lumpy, and she absolutely shone. She was wearing black leggings and a clingy pink sweater, and she looked ready for anything. I asked her what she had done to herself. She told me she was taking tap dancing, which she had excelled at as a girl. Resurrecting a childhood hobby was an obvious lift to this woman, and she said her husband thought it was great, too.

To the person you love, there is nothing more intoxicating than to have him never quite able to figure you out, to keep him guessing, curious. I used to knit as a teenager, and recently started again. Chuck shook his head in amazement when he saw me clacking away with needles and brown tweed yarn. "It's just not something I ever imagined you doing," he said. Grandmothers knit; the Iris he thinks he knows does not. When we are surprised by our partners, positive surprises, that translates into awe and respect. And that turns into a marriage that can remain interesting for decades beyond the fluttery newlywed phase.

As an oldwed, with not a perfect relationship but with growing love for my imperfect one, I look back at some of the abysses, the nights in the cage, when snarling animals nearly tore each other apart. And while I miss having snuggly, needy infants, I do not miss the dawn of our marriage, when, zonked from lack of sleep and angry over loss of self, I was more snappy than loving. Chuck wasn't at his best, either; in fact, as long as I'm beating myself up, this father of four babies was often unbearable to be around. Our time as a couple consisted mostly of barking logistics over the cacophony of wails, itemizing who would take what child to Tumble Tots, who would go to the pharmacy for pink antibiotics to treat an ear infection, whose turn it was to get up for the 4 a.m. feeding.

Leisurely and romantic, this new marriage was not. Frenetic and combustible, the relationship was more often than I'd like to admit. Torn between needy children and a needy spouse, I'd say, like a preschool teacher would tell a child, "We didn't use our nicest language." And we didn't share—another thing we require our children to do. We showered our children with love and were stingy with each other. Granted, when the babies start coming, they should be top priority. Infants and toddlers who are hungry and wet and who later routinely jump off tables demand to be attended to, sucking every last trickle of energy so that there is often nothing left to drizzle into the marriage. The kids are the winners, and the marriage loses out.

Here's something I learned from making some grave mistakes during those early years of being a wife and a parent: You should work on being as demonstrative in your love toward your spouse as you are toward your children. Husbands who are kissed and hugged often behave better. And, you should recognize early on that your marriage is the most important relationship in the family. The strength of the parent-child connection feeds directly off that. Ever notice how when we are harmonious in our marriages our children tend to be on a more even keel? On the flip side, when there's a lot of friction, kids are cranky and inconsolable.

I remember too many early evenings when Chuck would come home from work and I'd be bleary-eyed at the kitchen table, three kids in high chairs and one in a booster, and I'd be feeding them all something hot and delicious and homemade, dipping spoons into mouth after mouth after mouth after mouth, like tiny birds. Chuck would kiss us all on the head, and say, "Where's *my* dinner?" And I'd have to tell him there was nothing hot and homemade for him. After a twelve-hour day of zookeeping four sons, I frequently adapted a "fend for yourself" attitude when it came to catering to my own husband's basic needs.

And I paid the price. He felt neglected a lot of the time, then proceeded to neglect me, which made me angry a lot of the time. What we both really wanted and really needed at that hellish time of new marriage and new parenthood was to provide each other with a shoulder to lean on. But we were too mad and exhausted to humble ourselves and surrender. So what we got instead was the cold shoulder, hostility, bad fights, therapy bills. Some of my own anger came from seeing him come home from the office, in clean clothes, whistling, a bolo tie on, looking spiffy and relaxed. And I had just spent the day with sticky babies in a filthy house, my choice, yes, but grueling nonetheless.

As a wife who has come to understand the healing power of surrender and the importance of compromising instead of clawing, I wish I could redo the beginning of our marriage. There are plenty of blunders that still make me feel sad and bad; mistakes you can learn on my dime. I wish I had recognized that Chuck was going through his own set of hard changes with new fatherhood and new husbandhood. Over time, over wine, we have talked about how he was wincing for the old Iris who used to hold his hand at Sushi-Ko, and dance with him past midnight at clubs in Adams Morgan. He was sad that I seemed to care more about the children than I did about him, that he wished I could stay awake past 9 p.m.

And he was angry, too, that marriage wasn't what he expected it to be—a melding of two people who have vowed to be each other's partner, each other's lover, each other's ally. The truth is that although getting married and having babies are the most profound and fulfilling events of the life cycle, we were adversaries more than allies. I now see that, especially so in those first years when children are clamoring for us every second of the day, how crucial it is to pay attention to your husband. We have to muster up the strength, after force-feeding carrots to a toddler who hates them, to serve up something hot and homemade (carryout is fine) to a spouse just home from his own hard day. Cooking someone a meal is a simple way to show that we care; indeed, it's a universal way to someone's heart. I wish I had been a more nourishing partner to Chuck in those just-after-wedding-bam-into-diapers years, both in the foods served and the outpouring of time and affection.

The following woman reflects on her forty-year marriage and remembers, indeed, that simple acts such as walking and talking together, or putting lipstick on before a husband comes home, do strengthen the bond. Seven years ago, her husband died.

Dee is a stunning woman in her sixties, slim, with high cheekbones, a lilting voice that beckons and soothes. She lives outside Los Angeles, where she and her husband, Dick, an attorney who started his career as a clerk for Supreme Court Justice Felix Frankfurter, lived throughout their marriage, raising a son and a daughter. The Washington couple who directed me to Dee and Dick are diversely connected, high profile in their careers, and know lots of interesting couples in all pockets of the world. Of all these people, they describe this man and woman as having one of the very best marriages they had ever seen. Over a series of many conversations, here is what Dee revealed about what a good marriage feels like and what should go into the pot to make it good.

What made our marriage work for so many years? I did comb my hair and put on lipstick when I knew Dick was coming home, but of course, it's much more than that. At least one of you has to be centered, unruffled, and Dick was the rock of Gibraltar. I was the one making waves and searching; remember, most women of my generation didn't work, we volunteered and stayed home tending children.

We met right here in Beverly Hills, at a summer high school production of Outward Bound in which my little brother played Dick's grandson and sat on his lap. I was still wearing braids, no lipstick yet. I have a definite recollection of seeing him for the first time. He was a senior in high school when I was a freshman, and no one in the world will ever look as important to a freshman girl as a boy who is a senior in high school, as sexy and worldly. President Clinton doesn't look as important to me now as Dick did when I was a freshman in high school.

Therefore, from the very beginning of our relationship, I was sure that Dick was smarter than I was, and therefore had to be right. Marriage for me was a process of discovering that I was at least as right, if not more right, some of the time. Our life together wasn't a competition, but a process of listening carefully, and respecting—respect is a very important factor. You need to respect, as well as love each other. Respect to me means having an enormous regard for the integrity of your mate's opinions and ideas, and absolutely never belittling or shooting the other down.

The hardest part about being married to Dick was coaxing him to express his feelings; remember, this generation of men was disconnected from their emotions and their feelings. It was the most puzzling part of my marriage, to get this area to function. You know, when you get married you do not sit down with a syllabus: Making Marriage Work, semester one. We were so young when we got married, I was twenty-one and Dick had turned twenty-four the day before the wedding. Everyone was *getting married at this age. Looking back at it now, I see I was a child. We were children.*

In the 1950s, we married young, and generally did not have premarital sex, let alone live together before the wedding night. The way things are now, a prolonged period of living together and physical intimacy before marriage, that takes away the initial excitement of the first couple of years of marriage. It was so exciting when we got married, and could sleep together! That new toy can sustain a marriage for the couple of years until the babies are born, and then the thrill about babies takes over.

Now couples have eaten dessert first, and the excitement is dwindling just as they are getting married. But they are still not ready to have children, so they become somewhat bored with one another. Many marriages are on the brink of tedium right from the start. Then the babies come, and it's a total disruption of the parents' already fragile interaction, and the marriage collapses. So I'm not sure this process of living together, which is supposed to reveal so much about the person you are thinking about marrying, is actually beneficial to the institution of marriage. It has a definite down side; in our generation, when you got married, there was this sexy, wonderful discovery of each other.

My marriage lasted nearly forty years; Dick died seven years ago, just three months shy of our anniversary. Happiness is a very elusive quality, but I would say our marriage was rich, very rich. I worked on that richness, always trying to make our lives richer, not dollars richer, but more meaningful. If I were reliving my life I would start there. I would not try to make something that was already wonderful somehow more wonderful, more meaningful.

I see now that restlessness undermines feeling happiness in the moment. I thought if I worked harder, we could learn more, we could enlarge ourselves more. Really, it was ridiculous, we could have been sitting contentedly just looking at a flower. Yet Dick and I often raced around to learn about every possible thing that we could find. Now that he is gone I do wish there had been perhaps more savoring, more just sitting in his lap.

He died too soon, but he hadn't missed knowing his children. Once they were out of diapers, he was a totally involved father. He interrupted whatever he was doing to take their phone calls, and showed up at late-afternoon sports practices and games straight from the office in his gray flannel suit. Until they were in college, we never thought of traveling without them, and had wonderful learning experiences in Israel and India. We loved Indian art, and we wanted the children to share what we loved. We never stopped learning.

When we had a problem, I was fortunate that Dick would listen quietly to my dissecting, he would always hear me out. And then we would redirect the compass a little. There were never great redirections, just adjustments. He would fine-tune me and I would fine-tune him. You know, we grew each other up, and we grew up with each other.

People now marry in their mid to late thirties, when each person is well-defined, habit-ridden. How do you adapt your well-formed nature to another person? Yet, marriage requires really respecting what the other person needs. Marriage is not a contest of who is going to win the round. It's a delicate balancing of needs and costs to both parties.

I absolutely adored the way Dick's mind worked. He had an encyclopedic amount of information stored in his head, and could access it swiftly, and elegantly, in a sparse manner. He was rigorous in his approach to problem solving, which made him a very good lawyer. I found this seductive. It was as if, between the two of us, we made a whole person. Dick was intellect, and I, emotion. So I did the emoting for both of us, and he did the tough thinking, and between us it worked. It helped that we were in absolute harmony on what our goals were, for ourselves, for how we wanted to participate in the community, and for our children.

Neither one of us had a lot of time for buddying around with others, never. We were each other's best friends. And yes, there was romance. But I don't mean flowers, which he brought twice, each time I announced I was pregnant. We told each other we loved each other every day, every single day. When he died, I didn't have to feel guilty that he didn't know I loved him. I absolutely knew he loved me, and he absolutely knew I loved him.

Maybe this sounds goofy to you, that it was all so picture perfect, and of course it wasn't; there were days that I would be irritated because he said he'd be home at 6:30, and wouldn't arrive until 8:30. He had no sense of time, and there is no use in trying to change such a fundamental characteristic. You cannot. The quirks and peculiarities, which become even more pronounced as people age, have to be respected, even though you may not like them.

What about romance and sexuality in a long and happy marriage? Well, it's not like a hot love scene from a movie, but a deeper, much lower-volume kind of thing, not that blazing wattage. It is something that burns all the time, like a pilot light. It's always on, and from that—if you ever stop running around with your kids or your civic enterprises—you can get the fire started again. Dick and I used to joke that the real reason we sent the children to Sunday school was so that we could get in a couple of good hours together alone, while we were both awake.

So in the end, what do I recommend to singles? Change your expectations. Get realistic. If your standard is movie love scenes with perfect sex performed by gorgeous people, you will constantly be worried that you can't measure up. Nor would any partner. You would start out feeling cheated.

Dick was my other half, more than half, and it has been with great, great pain and effort that I have learned to live without him. I needed help in thinking, doing both parts of the dialogue myself. That was where I had to begin—to reach a point where I could decide something without talking it over. That was how we made life decisions—dialogue, the back and forth. It has been excruciating to learn to be the lone voice. And, as in the years when I pushed our marriage and our family to keep growing, I'm still demanding that of myself, I must keep growing to survive.

I have a passion for early Hindu and Buddhist art, and travel to remote sites in Asia. Especially thrilling now are my two young grandsons, and helping my daughter and son-in-law nurture the boys to become who they need to be. I think Dick would be pleased that I've come so far since his death, which was sudden and unexpected.

With luck, I could live another thirty years, but I cannot imagine spending all that time without Dick. Even with my wonderful children and grandchildren and friends, it is just so alone now. Our marriage, it was just one of those little miracles.

WHAT IS HAPPINESS?

I am thinking about Dee's line on happiness being an elusive quality, and how today she thinks the greatest joy may be found not from chasing around, but from being calm and still. Yet with children and jobs and the whirl of this world, it is difficult to create the calm necessary not only for individual happiness, but for a happy marriage.

"Do you know any couple that is really happy?" a girlfriend asks while we are having our daily parking lot conversation after drop-off at our children's school.

I tell her after talking to dozens of spouses about their satisfaction and malaise that my whole concept of happiness has changed, a state defined in the dictionary as "enjoying well-being and contentment." No husband or wife is happy all of the time; most are unhappy to some degree at least half of the time, few are happy most of the time. Happiness comes and goes in bubbles that last an hour, bursts that last a day, and if we're really on a roll, torrents that last a week. Happy for one whole month? Not a chance. We're too busy to be happy. Perhaps being happy in marriage is not what we should be seeking after all.

What I seek in marriage is what Jacob Needleman speaks of in *A Little Book on Love*: ". . . a miraculous sense of coming home. Home is where we can let down our guard. Here, finally we are safe." This home that houses a marriage needs to be constructed not of string and straw, but of concrete and steel, to withstand the grate and the grind of everyday life. The marriage house must be invincible enough to survive the centuries-old human condition of lusting for what you haven't got. Logan Pearsall Smith states it best: "There are two things to aim at in life, first get what you want, and after that, to enjoy it. Only the wisest of mankind achieve the second."

Look around you. Who is wise enough to really consider themselves happy? Who around you is satisfied with who they are and where they are at, and not itching to be somewhere, or someone, else? Since the start of civilization, we have aspired first to survive, and then to find happiness. We veer toward our relationships and possessions to get that high, and instead experience misery because people and things never fail to disappoint. People and things always fall short of our magnificent expectations. Buddhist masters wag a finger at us, warning us that we're looking in the wrong places to find bliss, that happiness is a construct of the mind, not something you get, or are owed, from the world.

In the Dalai Lama's book *The Art of Happiness,* His Holiness states, "I believe that happiness can be achieved through training the mind. . . . By bringing about a certain inner discipline, we can undergo a transformation of our attitude, our entire outlook and approach to living.

"In fact, whether we are feeling happy or unhappy at any

given moment often has very little to do with our absolute conditions but, rather it is a function of how we perceive our situation, how satisfied we are with what we have. . . . If you maintain a feeling of compassion, loving-kindness, then something automatically opens your inner door. Through that, you can communicate more easily with other people. And that feeling of warmth creates a kind of openness."

Love and happiness seem to flow constantly for the Dalai Lama because his mission is to light up darkness in others, and from that comes his own joy. And by living a life that is not of ego but of compassion and kind acts, we are saved from self-absorption and lamenting and blaming our malaise on someone else.

There is a lesson from *The Art of Happiness* to apply to marriage; to focus on what we give and not on what we think we should be getting. Yet, sublime selflessness is a difficult state to maintain in an everyday partnership, unless we are on a vacation in Tahiti or in an ashram meditating for hours on end. Most of us Westerners who have delved into Eastern traditions still feel the tug of our hardwired American beliefs; we worry that happiness is somehow still out there, dodging our grasp. We still don't get that there's no huge glob of cheese at the end of the maze, that instead, there are bits strewn all along the sides of the road.

"We try to obtain better material conditions, a better job, higher social status, and so forth; but no matter how successful we are in improving our external situation we still experience many problems and much dissatisfaction," writes Geshe Kelsang Gyatso in his *Introduction to Buddhism*. "We never experience pure, lasting happiness. . . . Buddha advises us not to see happiness outside ourself but to establish it within our mind. . . . If we train in this way we can ensure that our mind remains calm and happy all the time."

Calm and happy all the time? Do you know any couple,

even ones who meditate or pray faithfully, who fit that description? I'm thinking of one of the most outwardly calm couples I know. They are avid church goers, have been married forever, no children, tons of money. They summer in Italy, and the rest of the year live in a historic townhouse on Capitol Hill, where they eat dinner together every night by candlelight.

Despite their fortune, this wife is always yearning, for a better garden, a skinnier body, a more robust mind. The husband recently lost his father and has slumped into a blackness that has him drinking too much and snapping at his wife. Happiness in marriage, even for the tightest of couples, comes and goes in waves. This couple was happy most of the time for twenty years. Then, boom, the man is hit with the loss of his idolized father, his partner is hit by midlife malaise, and they shift into a darker place. We've been there. When Chuck's father died in March of 1994, we were rocked by our own black, bad slump. In grief, my husband understandably grew remote and distant, this at the precise time that Jack and Zane were born, joining brothers Theo, three, and Isaac, one. What I needed most at that point was a partner in the bedlam and what Chuck needed most was for me to leave him alone. We learned a lot about marriage during that period.

Going through hell is the reality of long-term relationships. To expect sustained happiness in marriage is a naive dream. We should expect, instead, periods of happiness broken up by loneliness, crying jags that come on for no apparent reason, even intolerable pain, and yes, bursts of sweet, sexy love. Knowing the dark side will make the good times all the more appreciated. Knowing the dark side has made me aspire not toward perpetual happiness but to being grounded, feeling safe, feeling sane, feeling like I am home. I am going not for high-pitched ecstasy, but for a steady hum.

Doing Transcendental Meditation, which I learned at age

nineteen in Boulder, Colorado, does help the hum along, putting things on more of an even keel. Chuck also does TM, and we talk a lot about trying to meditate together daily, and do so with part of our bodies touching each other. We know this would be healthy and unifying. So far, in twelve years, we've managed to meditate together three times. I feel like the tiny rubber Buddha my friend Milissa Murray bought me for my birthday. It's a woman Buddha, wearing a yellow robe, sitting in the lotus position, and in one hand she's talking on the cell phone, in the other hand she's holding a tall latte.

When Chuck and I do get our scarce moments alone, we'd rather be under the covers in a more rigorous form of meditation than sitting upright, atop our comforter. Sex does promote a calmer, more peaceful mind, and never fails to inject some happiness into marriage. Sex is a great item to put on a to-do list, on top of such things as "Buy Jack new P.E. shoes." Sex is a great healer, and it's also a whole lot of fun.

David Owen wrote a wickedly humorous article called "Here's a Really Great Idea" that ran in the October 27, 1999 issue of *The New Yorker*. The great idea is to have sex with your spouse once in a while.

As Owen prescribes:

> *If you've been married for a really long time, as I have, you probably don't need me to tell you that marriage can get a little boring after a while. Oh, boy, can it get boring. But it doesn't have to! There are quite a few little tricks and other things you can do to make it a lot more exciting and just plain fun. Here's one of them: having sexual intercourse.*
>
> *How much fun? Flying a kite, going to the circus, riding a horse, going out for ice cream—add all those things together and multiply by two. Seem like a lot?*

Sure does. But you're not even halfway to sexual inter-course.

Feeling bored? Having sexual intercourse is the perfect change of pace.

Perhaps as our sons mature and childcare duties dwindle, we will add "meditate together" to our list of to-dos. But not today; because we've gotta run. In the now, we are too busy in the flurry of the moment to savor the rippleless pond within. Today, in this moment, life is too crammed and crazy to stop and explain.

It was easier to be lulled into a meditative trance when the children were babies, and I was in my kitchen with other mothers, sipping coffee, rocking children. Time moved slowly, languorously. With nursing infants and streamlined careers, we basked in being where we were, when we were there. My own mother often tells me that the days she had her three young children around one kitchen table in Oak Park, Illinois, were the happiest days of her seventy-nine years. I think of her words when four boys have me stretching in dozens of directions, and I miss those days when they were in high chairs, and I was planted in front of them spooning food into tiny, pink mouths.

When I read my descriptions of being home with a puppy pack of little boys in *Surrendering to Motherhood*, it feels like I'm describing another woman. In this scene I am putting to-gether a zucchini quiche in our kitchen. This book was pub-lished in 1997, and I haven't made a quiche since.

As I wrote:

These I'm-at-One-with-the-Moments started to wash over me more often during new motherhood, twitters of calm when my mind would empty as I per-formed simple, necessary household chores. One came when I was scrubbing out stained baby bottles, a painstaking task that demands lots of wrist action with long-stemmed brushes. Another came when making zucchini quiche, when my consciousness shifts to my hands and the Pyrex bowl and the knife and how the deep green of the vegetables is the same mystical green of the pine trees out the window.

Throughout the process I realized I wasn't thinking of anything else—I was just moving my hands like a sculptor, pressing and forming and cutting. Quiche is a dish I make often and well, but something was different this December day. I wasn't rushing through it haphazardly; I was arranging it, alternating the right size slice of mushroom with a corresponding slice of zucchini, delicately sprinkling cheese as if tossing fairy dust, pouring the egg mixture slowly so it doesn't spill over the edges. Those quiches came out like cover shots for Gourmet, *their insides masterful masonry.*

I looked at my hands, etched with fissures from soapy water and Baby Wipes. I love the feel of these hands in mud or in child flesh or in brownie batter. I love how tranquility takes hold when the hands take over. I know what Ram Dass knows when he writes in Be Here Now: "It feels like the first real thing that's ever happened to me!" Everything else had a certain hustle like quality to it.

Those reflections on surrendering to motherhood make me wince for a bygone era, because the year 2000 has a hustle like quality to it, as we parent four school-age boys who play two and three sports each, guitar and piano and need rides there and back. Our marriage has a certain hustlelike quality to it as we push forward in artistic professions that we love and don't wish to pull back from. We, and most of the people around us, are multitasking on multiple tracks. Too busy doing, we are seldom just being, relishing our families clustered around a table, or taking fifteen minutes to snuggle with a spouse after an overwhelming day. Unfortunately, working at marriage often falls to the bottom of our to-dos, or never makes it on the list at all.

Driving to American University one morning with a bazillion to-dos banging around in my head, I looked at the tan Jeep crawling in traffic next to me. In it was a guy shaving while talking on his car phone. He looked back at me and his eyeballs seemed to be gyrating to the rhythm of his battery-powered razor. I have never shaved in the car, nor has Chuck, but we both have eyeball-gyrating days.

My millennium New Year's resolution: "Make time to move slower by moving slower yourself." So far, no luck. Just when I sit down, a child or a husband reminds me of something I didn't do and I pop up like a jack-in-the-box, to run our for a birthday present for a party that starts in an hour, to make a piano lesson that starts in fifteen minutes, to make dinner. I used to laugh when our middle son Isaac would ask me, breathless with anticipation about something he was about to do the next day, "Mommy, is it tomorrow yet?" Now when Isaac says that it makes me sad, because our days are so packed they often do blur together into a haze where yesterday seems indistinguishable from today, a blur where this month could just as well be two months ago.

In Mihaly Csikszentmihaly's groundbreaking book *Flow: The Psychology of Optimal Experience,* the author concludes after twenty-five years of research that the happiest people are those absorbed by creative and challenging professions, people wholly involved and flowing, mind and body, with their work. We achieve optimal joy, according to Csikszentmihaly, when "the action carries us forward as if by magic." Too often, however, that magic from all-consuming professions leaves little magic leftover for our spouses. Too much busyness often leads to unconsciousness, a state that can bring on ignorant bliss, and can also be a means of dodging the hard work it takes to solidify a marriage.

"Being superbusy all the time can be a way to avoid facing what you have to face," says New York psychotherapist Helene Brenner. "When you stop and really face yourself, or your partner, that can hurt. So rather than be depressed over some of the choices you have made in your life you replace that with overbooking yourself. That way, there is no risk of leaving any psychological space to look at what you really need to look at.

"When you're always moving, you never have to be truly present with yourself, or present in the experience of your marriage."

I'm listening to Al Green on my car radio romancing the restorative acts of walking and talking together in his song "Love and Happiness." And I'm reminded how easy it is to forget to even exchange a few cordial sentences with your partner in the course of a crazy day. I come home and am about to check my phone messages when Chuck reminds me that I have not spoken to him all day. I tell him that it's not like I'm ignoring him; I did make him dinner, his favorite, steak and mashed potatoes. He tells me that he'd rather have an Oriental chicken Lean Cuisine from the microwave if it meant he could have some of my attention.

I tell him that I can't sit with him right now because I have to return a couple phone calls and check my emails. He said he should come first and the rest can wait, and he is right. Loving someone at the moment they are asking for it because they need it even though you don't want to give it is the ultimate surrender in marriage. And it takes practice, discipline, just like any other art. When I make myself be still and really listen rapt as Chuck talks about his day, then fuss over him, rub his shoulders, he comes alive, he becomes very affectionate, we never argue on those nights. And all it takes is a little coddling to get those results; I often imagine what a whole year of being sweet would reap.

Chef Julia Child expresses one of her simple, sweet recipes for love in *Appetite for Life*, the biography of Child written by Noel Riley Fitch. Child says a happy marriage requires three ingredients, and they all start with the letter *F*. "Feed 'em, flatter 'em . . ." and I'll leave the third to your imagination. The three *F*s can indeed go a long way in perfecting the art of romance and relationship. In *The Art of Loving*, Erich Fromm offers further instructions on becoming an artist in matters of love:

". . . the mastery of the art must be a matter of ultimate concern; there must be nothing else in the world more important than the art. This holds true for music, for medicine, for carpentry—and for love. And, maybe here lies the answer to the question of why people in our culture try so rarely to learn this art, in spite of their obvious failures; in spite of the deep-seated craving for love, almost everything else is considered to be more important than love: success, prestige, money, power—almost all our energy is used for the learning of how to achieve those aims, and almost none to learn the art of loving.

"One will also recognize that while one is consciously afraid of not being loved, the real, though usually unconscious fear is that of loving," Fromm continues. "To love means to commit oneself without guarantee, to give oneself completely in the hope that our love will produce love in the loved person. Love is an act of faith, and whoever is of little faith is also of little love . . ."

Indeed, to admit that we love another is a real gamble, as we're setting ourselves up for anything when we say those words. Will the person love you back? For how long? Will it end up hurting? For all its wonders, love can be a big mess.

The first time Chuck Anthony told me he loved me he knew me for all of two weeks. I was getting on a United flight from Washington headed to San Diego because that afternoon my sister had telephoned to say "Daddy had a heart attack." It was a Sunday, and I had been on a date with Chuck the night before; I called him to ask him for a ride to the airport. He rushed over, helped me throw things into a suitcase, drove me to National Airport, then walked me onto the airplane, telling the flight attendant to take care of me. He then whispered in my ear, "I love you." Our relationship was too new to know whether I loved him back, and I was too scared that my father would die—which he did five weeks later—to even think straight and muster up anything to say in return. Yet, those words, *I love you*, were a great gift. Chuck gave me a spark of possibility, of hopefulness, to flicker on a five-hour flight into hospital hell, a spark that gave me warmth and life while facing the death of a person who I loved more than anyone else.

It was Chuck's act of faith to love someone suddenly and unwaveringly who couldn't love him back, and to stand by her until she would eventually wake up to the astounding goodness in the lovely and loving man who stood before her. I am still waking up.

What Is Love Anyway?

I love you. What does that even mean? "We were born for love. It is the principle of existence and its only end," Benjamin Disraeli said of love. Intimacy is the heart of existence, and love is the heart of intimacy. We need to feel connected to other people in a primal and abiding way; love makes us feel better, love makes us live longer, love makes us do the right thing. After being stripped down to what he called his "naked existence" in the Nazi concentration camps, where both his parents, his brother, and his wife were killed, Viktor Frankl came through his experience knowing he still wanted to live, because of his love for what was lost and his love for what could be. Frankl went on to become an author and psychiatrist who worked with despairing patients on reaching for reasons within for not committing suicide. As Frankl writes in *Man's Search for Meaning:*

"The uniqueness and singleness which distinguishes each individual and gives a meaning to his existence has a bearing on creative work as much as it does on human love. When the impossibility of replacing a person is realized, it allows the responsibility which a man has for his existence . . . A man who becomes conscious of the responsibility he bears toward a human being who affectionately waits for him, or to an unfinished work, will never be able to throw away his life. He knows the 'why' for his existence . . ."

An urge to complete a creative task, or to fulfill our commitments to a loved one, are compelling reasons to move forward, even when we feel like stopping and succumbing to depression. Viktor Frankl believed that the purpose of a human life is to search for meaning. The Dalai Lama believes the purpose of human life is to search for happiness. I believe we get married to find both meaning and happiness, but that throughout a lifetime, we never end up finding either full meaning or total happiness from anything or from anybody.

Because there are no ultimate answers, or as my eight-year-old Isaac says when I ask him a hard question, "Only the angels know, Mommy," I believe the best we can do to find happiness is to work every day at loving others and to work at jobs where we can be our most creative. I ask a popular Washington writer renowned for his ruminations on the elusive nature of happiness to talk about marriage. Sitting against shelves of philosophy books, in front of a black ashtray spilling over with Camel nonfilter butts, he talks about how joy can only be ours, in "little pieces," in a traditional life. Here is more from a man, married for fourteen years, father of twins, who wants to remain nameless so "my friends don't know how twisted I really am."

All my life I have noticed that after you meet someone or want something and you conquer them, then somehow it's never enough. For me, that means I'm always suffering because I always am desiring. You know how all the Eastern religions say you can stop your suffering if you stop the selfish desires of the ego. Well, they are right.

The way you achieve happiness is to give up wanting anything, which of course, is impossible. We are in the Western mode of desiring cars, big houses, diamonds, the most beautiful partner, nonstop great orgasms, and therefore we are doomed to be miserable, we are just totally screwed. Our Western culture programs us to think that if only we had all these things then ultimately we will be happy. But of course, all these things do not make you happy; having these things just makes you want more of these things.

Okay, so if that doesn't make you happy, then happiness must come from having a spouse and children and finding fulfillment in family. But, ultimately that doesn't work, either. The only thing that makes you happy is your own achievements. But that is short-lasting because then you have to keep achieving, doing something noteworthy, again and again and again. So at best, when you achieve something, you get to be happy for a day. That's all we get. We get happiness in little pieces, it gets measured out for us in tiny fragments that we can savor, but then the feeling leaves us. What is happiness then? Happiness becomes not something we experience, but something we remember, a memory of a high from a time that is now gone.

Let's talk about the happiness that comes from a longstanding, dependable marriage. It's a subtle happiness, not the roar or intensity so many of us desire. We all know people who go for the roar, chase the hot romance, the hot affair. But that, too, is an illusion of happiness; part of the charm of an affair is that it is inaccessible and impermanent, it's just a dream. As human beings, it is part of our makeup to crave the forbidden, the dangerous. But once we get the forbidden, the fruit isn't so sweet. As human beings, we have to control our sexual urges, but we cannot control our sexual urges. Over the course of thousands of years, we have seen how the powerful urge for passion and sex and romance can cause complete social anarchy unless it is controlled. There is no more powerful force on earth. Sex is the white-hot core of human beings, especially when it is unrequited. You remember Truman Capote's great line in his book Answered Prayers: *"There are more tears shed over answered prayers than over unanswered ones."*

In marriage, even the best ones, you know you should feel full and happy, but often you reside in a state of emptiness. You are busy with a job, but instead of feeling fulfilled, you feel overwhelmed. You know your partner loves you, yet you feel underappreciated. Some people may choose to fill their emptiness with another person. They think, If only I could possess her then I would somehow feel better because it would take me out of myself. *They see erotic joy as a solution, only to find out the solution was temporary, that they were temporarily escaping their responsibility, temporarily escaping the burden that being a spouse and raising a family puts on your soul, and on your psyche. And getting what you want makes everything worse. Then the new person started needing you, too, and it becomes just another burden.*

It's the hardest thing in the whole world to live one ordinary life without cracking it up. It's a miracle that we as human beings can go through our one life without destroying someone, without murdering someone, without fleeing our families. I used to read about all the inner-city killings and parents who abandoned children in the Cityside section of our newspaper and think, Oh my, how did all these lowlifes create such messy, messy lives around them? But with age I know that you and I are no different than them; we just are better at containing the way we escape from our ordinary lives. We are better at fighting our own self-destructive urges. These other people can't control their rage, the selfish human desires we all have to destroy, to be free. I accept that I will never be completely happy. I accept that there may be soul mates out there who may forever be unknown to me.

The One Who Got Away

Perhaps, as the flawed human species we are, we can never escape the glance over a shoulder toward a life that was possible, but never materialized, for one reason or another, distance, timing, fate. I talk with girlfriends about old boyfriends, "the ones who got away." Lost loves? We all have them. Can we ever lose them totally?

A black-and-white photograph falls out of my college dictionary, frayed at the edges, faded and creased. Yet, the face is indelible, with its lopsided grin that still zonks me a lifetime later. A lock of hair falls over his eyes, like it always did when we walked the northern California beaches that summer of 1976, the summer we were inseparable, intoxicated by a first love so intense I couldn't eat, couldn't sleep, couldn't do anything but be with him.

In the summer of 2000, holding a small son's feet in the surf on a beach on the other side of the country, a magnificent husband by my side, the salty air hits my cheek in a way that slaps me back into that moment with the One Who Got Away, the one who loved Fleetwood Mac and took me from girl to woman. He was the twenty-two-year-old left behind in Santa Monica nearly a quarter of a century ago, but time has failed to erase.

What is it with old loves? Just when we have finally forgotten them, which may take decades, something happens, the throb of the ocean, a snapshot found in a drawer, and we're back at college graduation, when the two of you swore you'd get back together someday, this time forever, after you made something of yourselves, and saw something of the world. Years passed and one person's head got turned in another direction, and the other person got tired of waiting and now, here you are, spending forever with someone else.

But the One Who Got Away still makes us wince. He still haunts us in an occasional dream. We hate ourselves for being compelled to locate him through detective software designed to "find anyone, anywhere," and our chests tighten when his name comes up on the computer screen, complete with email address. Should you send a friendly greeting?

"Hi, remember me? I was once the love of your life. What's happening?"

I'll never forget when Mr. California called sixteen years ago to tell me he was getting married. I didn't want to marry him but I didn't want anyone else to marry him, either. When I hung up the phone, there was a burn in my gut. That conversation signified the end chapter in an ever-mysterious, always-tantalizing, on-again, off-again relationship that for a decade danced in the spirit of "someday, maybe." Now, he was really gone and in essence, my girlhood felt officially over.

We were able to move on, with new partners we love, and build families on opposite coasts. I have four sons, he has three sons, and we are blessed, I know. Often, the demise of a monumental romance can keep us from growing and loving, we become stuck in what was, even if what was wasn't all that great. Bethesda psychologist Jim White calls this obsession the "what-if syndrome."

"It's an unrequited love which the person did not have an opportunity to live out," White explains. "The person then goes through his or her life wondering, 'What would it have been like? Would it be better than what I have right now?'

"Of course, an unfulfilled fantasy is always more seductive than real life," adds White. "But there's only a first time once. And that first time in love is so powerful, it leaves a permanent mark on the memory."

Debbie Glasser, a mother of three teenagers in Potomac, Maryland, met her first love freshman year of high school in Oak Park, Illinois. She was a cheerleader, he was a football star. They went steady for a year and a half, spending every day after school together, and every Friday, Saturday, and Sunday night.

"He was my first real kiss, and my first real everything else," Glasser says of the boy who abruptly broke up with her junior year, leaving her for another girl, an apple-cheeked soprano in the high school choir. Being abandoned at the age of sixteen by her first love was an emotional jolt Glasser still feels at forty-seven.

"It was so painful that I never wanted to feel that same kind of love again," says Glasser. "I started choosing my boyfriends for different reasons, such as being a nice person or being stable, rather than gravitating toward romances with magic."

Throughout her decade-long marriage, which ended in divorce, and subsequent serious relationships, Glasser has been unable to shake the startling love she once felt. Several years back, she tracked down her high school prince to see if there was anything left between them.

"He had a long, braided ponytail and was living on a farm

raising goats," laughs the woman dressed in Versace. "Thank God I found out we had grown in separate ways."

Yet, Glasser never threw out their crushed, dried corsages from homecoming and prom, She just looked at them the other day, fingering the petals with French-manicured nails, remembering each event as if it happened yesterday, not thirty years ago. "How could I get rid of these things?" she asks in a whisper.

In 1956, at Walter Johnson High School in Bethesda, Maryland, Dan Shaver met a young girl he calls "the love of my life" in English class. Shaver mourned silently for Stacey for decades to come, after his family moved to New Jersey during their junior year.

"I thought about her every single day," says Shaver, during four years at Dickinson College and throughout his twenty-two-year marriage. "That didn't help matters in my marriage," he admits of a relationship that produced two children, now in their early thirties. Newly divorced and still stuck on Stacey, Shaver mustered up the courage to call her after twenty-four years of no contact. He was living in St. Louis and she was living in Middleburg, Virginia, divorced, single, with no children. They agreed to meet for dinner in Washington, a long meal at the Jockey Club that led to other long meals and weekends.

"When we started talking, right away it felt very comfortable, very easy, like time had stood still," says Shaver. "In my heart, I knew that Stacey and I belonged together the whole time we were not together." They married in September of 1986, overlooking the eighteenth hole of the golf course in Pebble Beach.

During their years apart, Stacey also sensed an intuitive rightness about the boy with the flat-top buzz cut she loved at first sight. "I was devastated when he moved away in high school. We were madly in love. When he called me out of the blue and announced, 'This is a voice from your past,' I said, shaking, 'Dannnnny?' I was so excited. I never thought I would see him again. But on another level, I always knew we were meant to be together."

Maud Lavin and Locke Bowman, girlfriend and boyfriend during three years of Harvard in the early 1970s, fell back in love in their forties after an urgent and erotic reunion in cyberspace. He was a divorced lawyer with two sons living in Chicago; she was a divorced writer with no children living in New York. A friend put them back in touch and they decided to have dinner, their first date in twenty-two years. Awash with sexy memories, they began courting through email; hot, bold, tender dispatches, amplified and electrified by electronics.

Here's a snippet of how their email correspondence "avalanched," in their words, into falling in love again.

> To Locke from Maud: "What I'd really like is just to see you again . . . talk a lot, joke around, flirt, not jump into bed (sorry), have a good time. (Well, I would like to jump into bed, and I'm very sure it would be wonderful, but not out of the blue, not quickly, not torn from what could be a luxurious and sensual series . . .)"

> To Maud from Locke: "Does this happen to you a lot? Getting into this kind of an email relationship? I want to see your face and taste your mouth . . . and know you again. I want it to last forever."

> To Locke from Maud: "I want to love and be loved. I want passion, and I want cuddling and tenderness. I eventually want . . . to remarry. . . . After finally feeling deeply again, I don't want to put myself on hold in a long-distance, yearning, can't-have-him mode. I decided to take the risk and tell you what I'm feeling."

> *To Maud from Locke: "I'm rushing this out just to say that I have been feeling all the things you were describing in your email and I lie awake at night and think about you . . ."*

Maud Lavin and Locke Bowman were married on April 16, 1997 in Chicago's City Hall.

Reflecting on their second chance at romance and commitment, Maud has this to say: "To be in love as kids, then again as adults, it's very heady, there's a lot of warmth, a lot of humor, a lot of loyalty, a lot of respect for each other on how far we've come. That person knows exactly who you are."

I ask Maud if being in love with someone at forty-five who she loved at nineteen makes her feel like a perpetual teenager.

"In a way, the eroticism and playfulness makes you feel young, but we're very aware that we are middle-aged now," says Maud. "I do not feel like a teenager, but I do feel lucky. It's very nice to grow old with the person who was your first, big love."

I could not have grown old with any earlier boyfriends because while there was big love, there wasn't mature love. Chuck and I are connected, somehow, in our deepest and oldest place. We are soul mates, whatever that is. Listening to the above stories on lost-and-found loves I can't stop mulling over this vague concept of "soul mate" our generation has relentlessly, obsessively pursued. What does soul mate mean, really? Someone you meet, soul to soul? Who can you genuinely touch in that way, really, other than God? Before I was married I consulted a psychic in San Francisco because I thought I found my soul mate, but this so-called soul mate hadn't realized it. The suspense was driving me nuts.

The psychic told me that I was my soul mate so I should stop looking for one. Me? My own soul mate? It began to make wonderful sense, that what we often seek is a mirroring of who we are in the form of another person. And when we find that person who will say, "Yes, you are tops, one in a zillion," it feels like a filling of the soul but it's really a filling of the ego. We should learn to bask in the fullness of a "Me" without a mirror, something that could keep us from expecting fullness to come from some unknown "You" out there. This advice from a psychic made all the difference in the world when it came to adjusting expectations in finding a partner. A spouse is someone you meet shoulder to shoulder, nose to nose, someone you should be able to deal with in the physical universe, someone you want to climb all over. A spouse is a real person, and not necessarily an ephemeral link to the soul. My husband is the man I crash into when I'm tearing through the house trying to find a missing black Adidas or the last Corona.

I asked Chuck if he thought I was his soul mate and he said, "Sure." I asked him how he knew for sure. And he said what he always says: "Because you are my wife," and continued watching the Washington Capitals get beat on TV. Chuck is not a wordy kind of guy, but what he says generally cuts to the core. I am his wife, a mate on all levels, right down to the soul, as evidenced in our mystical composite creations, Theo and Isaac and Jack and Zane, with their lanky bodies and wiry hair and blue-green eyes. These children are the embodiment of two souls melding, a family we can hang on to, something real, something we can never rearrange or change. We are stuck, and that is good.

A good marriage becomes an easy rhythm between partners, a gentle sway that takes years of cohabitation to choreograph and synchronize. A good marriage is two people in one house, knowing when to touch and knowing when to leave each other the hell alone. This dance, however slow and robotic and familiar, is better than spinning around with a carousel of new lovers who make you dizzy with ecstasy because they never stick around long enough to get old. It's easy to idealize a new lover, and think them the mate of our soul. Erich Fromm characterizes this worshipful new love in *The Art of Loving:* "This idolatrous love is often described as the true, great love; but while it is meant to portray the intensity and depth of love, it only demonstrates the hunger and despair of the idolater . . ."

Most of us who once had active dating lives know the hunger and despair that comes with wanting to possess someone we believe has the goods that will fix our lives. Of course, no one can do that. The psychic I consulted was right on when he said my soul mate was me, meaning the hunger to be spiritually whole should be fed from within. From that point, we can create a healthy relationship with another, based not on a childish neediness, but on a pairing of intact adults. Yet, we can't help but question whether what we're getting from our partners is enough as we listen to our friends reflect on their own marriages.

I am sharing a bottle of cabernet with Elspbeth and Mary, after spending all day writing about husbands and wives and other imperfections. Neither of these women, friends who also have young children, has any angst about their relationships on this night; in fact, they were giddy about their husbands. I listened to their valentines and it enlarged my own feelings of being adrift at this moment in May when Chuck is on a bad architectural deadline to finish a school project, and he is stressed and aloof.

My friends and I are at the Chart House, with a view of the Chesapeake Bay, and we are looking at small sailboats racing, each with one skipper, and I am feeling like those sailors, alone, in a vast sea. Yet, I know that loneliness will most likely be replaced with a whole new set of feelings the following day, that the trick in marriage is to "swing with it," something my father used to tell me to do when obstacles came my way.

I run into Mary the next morning at our children's school and tell her how jealous I was the night before hearing about her domestic bliss. She smirked and said: "Well, we should go out again tonight. Things are rotten today." And, as it turned out, as the day unfolded for me things were not nearly as rotten as they had been yesterday. And so it goes, five steps forward, three steps back. All you can do is hang on for the ride, a ride that is alternately rough and smooth, a ride that takes you through bushes and brambles, over jagged boulders and smooth pebbles, a road where the terrain is never the same from lope to lope. You swing with it, that's all you can do.

I'm talking to Rueben, very short, very droll, a college professor from Boston. Married and sixty-two, he has had several affairs, one intense, yet he is committed to staying married to his spouse of thirty-three years. They just celebrated their wedding anniversary with a trip to the Seychelles Islands off the coast of Africa. We were seated next to each other at a table for a mutual friend's sixtieth birthday party, and he asked me what I did. When I told him I was an author working on a book called *Surrendering to Marriage,* he got the strangest expression on his face. He became white, his lips pursed, his eyes wide, then he snorted and sighed.

Rueben said that he knew a lot about marriage; that over the years he had stretched the boundaries of marriage about as far as any one person could stretch them. But, he had never "broken out," and he was eager to describe his struggle to make his marriage work. We met the following week to continue the conversation. Here is what he told me.

There have been many periods over thirty-three years when I have thought about getting a divorce. I have been with other women who I found more attractive, who I was sure would be more satisfying. I was with one woman for a long time who I passionately believed would be more fulfilling to be married to; as if she were my other half I lost at birth. But the fact of the matter is that when you are married, your relationship with any-one else is by its very nature artificial.

This woman was twenty years younger than me, an ambi-tious, sensuous, young woman who adored me. Who doesn't want that? But as far as genuinely knowing each other—we didn't have to develop parenting skills together like my wife and I have had to do for our three children. We didn't have to negoti-ate how a limited amount of money is going to be spent. We don't know each other's bad or petty habits.

We had no agenda other than to make each other happy. In marriage there are a thousand issues you have to deal with all the time, and making each other happy gets lost.

I've had enough therapy to realize that the reason I keep looking around goes back to my relationship with my mother, and not feeling loved by her. You meet a woman who makes you feel loved, and it's blissful. But, as time passes, her love never fills the void left by your mother. It becomes an addiction. After a while you don't feel loved enough by the new woman, and so you keep looking for someone else who will love you even more. After oodles of therapy, I have come to know that this is my problem, and I am not alone. When you are incapable of feeling loved, nothing will scratch that itch.

You can chase other women with the fantasy that each one will make you complete, but they cannot, no one can. If you imagine the world from an infant's point of view, an infant has only two real desires. One, that they be fed. And the other is that they not be abandoned. I suspect that all men grow up with a profound fear of being abandoned by their mothers and when they become adults they transfer that fear onto their wives. The reason I have not left my wife in the end is because I don't want her to abandon me. I know that sounds insane, that I won't leave *her so she won't abandon me, but that's how it is for me and probably for thousands of other men.*

I was caught in this affair and although that was horrible, I think it actually led to having a better marriage. Having to be honest about this inevitably leads to a discussion over what the problems were, and we got to re-create the relationship. Most of the men I know have had at least one affair, and I can tell you hands down, their marriages turn out better when their wives find out because then you have to swim around in a real situation and make real changes.

When my wife found out, she did not ask me to leave, although the confrontation and conversation was very painful. Why didn't she kick me out? Why should she trash her life because her husband has put his penis in the wrong place? Was what really happened so serious that she's going to give up her house and her security, and give up companionship with someone she essentially loves? And I didn't leave basically because I knew deep down that she really did love me and my problems might be far worse with another woman. Many of the problems in my marriage were of my own doing, and they would come up again. I was tempted, yes, but wise enough not to make a move.

You know, I'm in my early sixties, and I have abandoned the fantasy that I'm going to find the other half of my soul in someone else. I've become very content with the idea that I'm married and I'm going to stay married. You're not going to like this, but that doesn't mean I wouldn't follow through on an opportunity with another woman to get momentary sexual pleasure again. But I'm not going to expect her to fill my dreams for a lifetime.

Life is good with my wife and I know that I'm incredibly lucky. Most people have no concept of how good their lives are.

Last night I was out for dinner with a guy friend of mine and we're at this restaurant where the hostess had the most fabulous body. I couldn't keep my eyes off her. I told my friend, "She is so sexy, I'm madly in love with her." He told me to put it out of my mind—*"What do you have to offer her?"* And it's true; what do I have to offer her? I could screw her. I could offer her my scintillating conversation. But she's my childrens' age. How much of my life's experience can she really understand? She would always come second to my family.

And what do I get? A young woman who might worship me for a while, but with whom I have almost nothing in common. She is no companion for life. The companion I do have knows me better than anybody. She accepts me and loves me with whatever flaws I have. I know that she will take care of me, and is someone who is essentially on my side.

I don't think sex is that important in the longevity of a marriage. Intimacy is, to the extent that it means sharing emotions and allowing yourself to feel vulnerable. At my age, after thirty-three years, sex in a marriage isn't the hottest of hot. We are companions, that's the most important thing. If people in their twenties and thirties think that sounds sad, that's their inexperience talking. There is nothing sad about having someone with whom you are totally comfortable.

My shrink used to tell me when I thought I was in love with that young woman, *"You are not really in love with her. You are in love with the feeling you get when you are with her—she makes you feel good about yourself. If you felt good before you went into the bedroom with her, you wouldn't need anyone to give you that feeling."* And the shrink was right. The trick to all of this is to feel whole with who you are, for you to love yourself.

Rueben and I talked more about self-acceptance and self-love as crucial in being a solid partner for someone else. He says that the older he gets, the harder it is to change, but the easier it is to count his blessings at home. I read him my favorite paragraph from the book *Embracing Each Other* by Hal Stone and Sidra Winkelman: "If we wish to surrender to the process of consciousness, we must surrender to it in all its complexities and contradictions. If we want to be loving human beings, we must learn to love our own wolves and jaguars and snakes and dragons, and stupidity and irritability and weakness and vulnerability and darkness as much as we love our loving and rational, competent, caring, and light-oriented selves."

I pick up John Updike's book *A Month of Sundays* to get some further insights on what drives people with solid marriages into adultery. The main character, Thomas, is a Christian minister who has repeated affairs with female parishioners because, as he puts it, he suffers "from nothing less virulent than the human condition . . . the malady is magnificent." One of his lovers tattles, and Thomas is shipped away by the church to a rehabilitation retreat where he delivers sermons in his imagination, explaining the mess he has gotten himself in.

Here is how Thomas rationalizes his unholy behavior:

For what is the body but a swamp in which the spirit drowns? And what is marriage, that supposedly seamless circle, but a deep well up out of which the man and woman stare at the impossible sun, the distant bright disc, of freedom?

Wherein does the modern American man recover his sense of worth, not as dogged breadwinner . . . but as romantic minister and phallic knight, as personage, embodiment, and hero? In adultery. And wherein does the American woman, coded into mindlessness by household slavery and the stupefying companionship of greedy infants, recover her powers of decision, of daring, of discrimination—her dignity, in short? In adultery.

The adulterous man and woman arrive at the place of their tryst stripped of all the false uniforms society has assigned them; they come on no recommendation but their own, possess no credentials but those God has bestowed, that is, insatiable egos and workable genitals. They meet in love, for love, with love; they

tremble in a glory that is unpolluted by the wisdom of the world;
they are, truly, children of lights. . . . The sheets of the marriage
bed are interwoven with the leaden threads of eternity; the cloth
of the adulterous couch with the glowing, living filaments of
transience. . . ."

John Updike's defrocked preacher believes that Jesus in-
stituted marriage as an "eternal hell" from which adultery is
the means to escape to "a galaxy of little paradises." Yet, people in the cushions of adulterous couches rarely describe their
extramarital liaisons as paradises, or reasons to rejoice. God
has a better way to allow husbands and wives to connect with
other interesting, challenging, attractive males and females—
flirting. A flirty friendship outside of marriage need not enter
the danger zone, where clothes come off and boundaries are
crossed and hearts get destroyed and lives explode. Flirting can
just be flirting; clean, revitalizing fun.

When a flirtation is played out right, we get a friend for
life instead of a short-lived lover. It may take every ounce of
human will to do the right thing when faced with an intense
chemical attraction to someone off limits. I'm speaking to Suzanne, a forty-two-year-old woman from Naples, Florida, a
mother of one child, the wife of a health club owner. She has
never strayed from her marriage, a volatile partnership with a
man who works long hours and can be incommunicative.
During the past year, one of the husbands they are both close
to in their social circles of couples has become more than a
friend to her. Thus far, they have been able to keep their emotional affair at the flirty, friendship stage; they have never even
kissed. She is fearful that if she even takes a tiny step toward
expressing the enormous affection she feels for this man that
she will not be able to stop. They joke about how they'll get
together in twenty years, and grow old together, this after their
own children are settled and grown.

I have seen them together, and the way they look at each other, the urgency of their conversation, is to know that there are hundreds of things far less possible than for these two people, each married to another, to end up together someday. Here is her story:

I have a very comfortable relationship with my husband, and it took a long, long time to develop that comfort level. I know that it would take years and years to duplicate this. Yet there is this unbelievable excitement with this other man, my heart literally goes pitter-patter. I get pangs, butterflies, the most amazing of feelings. I don't remember ever having that with my husband, that desire. There is an element of magic I've never had before. And whether or not this man is my soul mate, I have my doubts about that concept, I feel very lucky to know this feeling. It is a love I have not yet had before.

But I haven't crossed the line, even with this heart-stopping feeling, this absolute and total connection. I think of him as my intellectual mate, and my emotional mate, and sexually, oh my God. Sometimes I'm driving in my car and imagining that I'm having sex with him. When I'm in my kitchen I imagine that I'm kissing him. I am unbelievably drawn to this guy, he is smart, sexy, terrific. And so there is mental anguish that goes along with being involved emotionally, regardless of whether or not you have crossed the line. What is really crossing the line? Once you have fallen for this other person, and are connected emotionally, those feelings don't just stay in check because you haven't kissed the man. And when you are dealing with these intense feelings, it is almost impossible for it not to affect the level of intimacy with your own spouse. When you are angry with your husband, you feel yourself gravitating to the other. When things are good with your husband, you are only temporarily okay.

And I do imagine that one day we may cross the line, al-

though I do everything in my power not to. One day he dropped me off and he massaged my neck lightly, and I just froze. That was the first and last time he touched me; he gets it that we cannot do that right now, although I know if I made a move he would be more than receptive. But I have set up very strict boundaries and we both know it. If I kissed him just once, I know that this is someone I could fall madly in love with. This is not an infatuation because I actually know him very well. It is reality based.

I speak to him every single day on the telephone, sometimes twice a day, sometimes five times a day, and some of our conversations last for a long time. We talk about serious subjects, but there is always an element of fun, of flirtatiousness. Now, there are days that go by that I don't talk to my husband, but not this man—we always check in with each other.

So, yes, I'm on the edge here, within my boundaries, which I can tell you are hard to keep. I have not crossed the line, and it takes a lot of strength, I'll tell you. How can I stay on this side of the line? Because it would destroy my marriage and tear apart my family.

But I do imagine that once his kids are older and my kids are older we will end up together. Even though it hasn't happened, there already is this fusion of passion, and it has been very confusing at times. Luckily, I have a place to go to every week, to my shrink, and she keeps me honest. I basically tell her everything. If I could hide behind my actions there might be more of a tendency to misbehave. But this way, I'm accountable. I have to report in every week.

So, I'm a married woman with a husband who loves me, and I have this amazing chemistry with someone else. It feels like this is the person I was destined to be with, and I've felt that way almost from day one. Yet, I'm no fool. I know that living with him could drive me up a wall. But none of that diminishes this overwhelming feeling I have of love, and of rightness. I'm just doing my very best to stay on this side of the line.

It can take great fortitude to keep from stumbling over the line, to keep from surrendering to the throb of loins. But when lust stays in the heart, we get to retain the purity and perfection of the dream of that other person. The dream of "what if?" is nearly always more beautiful than the imperfect creatures and impure situations that emerge when the boundaries are crossed. Sometimes all it takes is one make-out session to dissolve the fantasy. After a bad first kiss, feelings of lust and love can easily turn out to be like a tropical storm that blows in and blows out.

Long ago, I had a monstrous crush that felt like love on a Mr. Perfect who appeared to have everything. He was tall and he had the face of Michelangelo's *David*, his hair was black, wavy and thick. He played tennis and played impossible to get, making him, of course, all the more desirable. He knew history, he knew art, he knew stocks, he knew Schramsberg champagne, an obscure nectar that happens to be my favorite.

When I met him he was about to become engaged to a woman he wasn't sure he wanted to marry, which made me sure he should be marrying me instead. The more he wavered, the more certain I became that we were meant to be. My anxiety propelled me to run more miles than I had ever run before in back of the National Cathedral near my apartment in Washington. During sleepless nights, I devised schemes to get the ungettable. One Saturday morning, he called early to tell me, "You have won." Strange choice of words I see now, pointing more toward love of self than love of me. But, at twenty-eight, single and searching, his declaration of himself as the grand prize sent me flying. He then invited me to breakfast at a pancake house.

I sped to the restaurant dressed for mischief, and we sat

in a corner booth and just stared at each other, unflinching, our irises locked, as if in a trance. So this was it, the real thing. My parents had always told me, "Don't settle when it comes to love," meaning go for the gold, not the bronze. And this feeling of rightness at this moment with this man was the gold, he was the biggest fish, this was first-string love. Yes, I had won, indeed.

We ordered bacon and buttermilk pancakes and pushed the food around on our plates, eating nothing while our eyes said everything. I remember there was a dribble of blueberry syrup on my thumb and I kept rubbing it with my index finger, trying hard to concentrate on the stickiness and the sensation of flesh on flesh, to keep centered, to keep me from shrieking crazily.

At my car, my dream man, who I was now certain I would marry, said good-bye with kiss, a kiss that started out with the feeling like every cell in my body had been torched. But the kiss went on long enough for me to notice a slight taste of tobacco, just a wee taste, but enough to know that Mr. Perfect smoked and I detest cigarettes, and you know, it was enough to douse the fire, just like that.

"What's wrong," he asked when I pulled away.

"You smoke," I said.

"Yes. But I'm trying to quit," he said back. Call me narrow, ridiculous, but the kiss that tasted like cigarettes made me fall out of love—instantly. I can't be with someone who is "trying to quit" cigarettes. I hate smoking, and told him so. On the ride back to my apartment, listening to Diana Ross sing "Seeing you only breaks my heart again," I thought about the uneaten pancakes I was suddenly starving for, and the mortal who wasn't a Michelangelo god after all. I thought about how I must look to him—overly reactive, inflexible. I thought how nasty habits lay beneath all our impeccable facades—nail biting, teeth gnashing, smoking, being too judgmental—quirks that are revealed over the course of time and not immediately apparent on the pretty faces we show to strangers.

This man and I never had another date, and so ends the story of the Big Tuna who in a fingersnap became a slithery sardine I didn't want to keep because of a long kiss soured by a Marlboro. I ran into him fifteen years later, and he told me he had married the woman he was almost engaged to when we met, and that he still wasn't sure if she was the right woman for him. They have two teenagers and he still smokes, but he said he was trying to quit.

I told him that what I was discovering, more solidly every day, was that the surest way to be happy in marriage is not to think too much about whether or not we are happy. My own marriage feels best when I'm living it and not analyzing it, when I'm swinging with it and not stuck in doubt or ambiguity. "Being present—rather than being emotional—is what allows real intimacy to happen," writes John Welwood in his book *Love and Awakening*. And he is right—marriage shifts from day to day and we must ride loose in the saddle, in a state of wakefulness, with a sense of humor.

It's 7:38 a.m. on a Monday, and I'm in a checkout line at the pharmacy to pick up some medication for poison ivy. My house is a mess, the children are on summer vacation, and I'm grumbling to myself about Chuck, who is right now drinking coffee that I made, eating eggs that I scrambled, and reading *The Washington Post* I fetched for him from the mailbox. I asked him before I left to have the boys make their beds and to please make ours. I also asked him to please—I did say please—pick up the mounds of his shirts and his pants that cover the chair and couch and floor in our bedroom.

Driving home after a forty-minute wait at the Rite Aid, I am getting angrier and angrier as I inch closer to the home where I know a sprawling mess awaits me, not only the un-made beds, the clothes to pick up, but now the egg-encrusted breakfast dishes that are piled in the sink. As I stomp into the doorway, I crunch the leg of a Buzz Lightyear toy. "Boys, I'm home," I yell, going from filthy room to filthy room. No one answers, and I hear no sounds. I look into each bedroom and still can't find the boys and Chuck. There are terry-cloth bath-robes and pajamas on the couch; oh good, at least he got them dressed. Still steaming, I yell once again, "Chuck!" And six-year-old Zane answers, "Mommy, we're in the attic," the place where we have a big, toy-filled playroom. I climb the stairs, ready to sputter, and find architect Chuck directing the con-struction of what is a nearly finished eight-foot skyscraper of Legos.

Chuck is on his knees putting a little man, who Zane tells me is a window washer, midway up the structure. Then my husband says, "We used every Lego we have," and I don't know who seems the most excited about the mini-Sears Tower of plastic blocks, the forty-three-year-old project manager or his crew of four young boys. I swallow my list of "why didn't yous" and quickly quit fuming, swelling with gratitude as I remember all the reasons I thought Chuck would be a good husband and father when I met him, and seeing my instincts were right. I don't have a clean house, ever. But I do have a husband who is patient and artistic and loves kids.

I slink down the stairs, make all the beds, and even do the unthinkable—I hang up all of Chuck's clothes, clothes I swore to him I would never hang up and he could just let pile up until he had nothing left to wear. I think of the time years ago when I was complaining to therapist Ruth Berlin that Chuck never hangs up his clothes. I asked her what I should do. She told me to hang up his clothes, which would be a good exercise for me in the practice of loving-kindness.

At the time, I got very defensive and told her I would

never hang up his clothes because it would only make him expect me to keep doing it. I told her I live in a house full of boys and I didn't want our males to grow up thinking that housework was a female thing, a wife thing. I insisted that Chuck, who was middle-aged, should hang up his own clothes; I hang up mine, and I ask the children to fold and hang up theirs. Ruth insisted, "Hang up his clothes. It will be good for you. It will be good for the two of you."

As usual, Ruth was right. By putting forth that small gesture of compassion, hanging up piles that my husband doesn't want to deal with, Chuck acted as if I had just written him a check for $10,000. He hugged me hard, kissed me hard, told me it made him feel taken care of; I'm serious, he went nuts. And you know, it *was* good for us. It was good for me to do something I really didn't want to do but did anyway because I knew it would make Chuck happy. And I saw how easy it can be to make a husband happy; really, it's the little things that can reap the biggest rewards.

When I take care of Chuck in subtle ways, cook him a steak his favorite way—black on the outside, rare in the center—he in turn does things for me, tells me a dress looks great, or sweeps the kitchen.

Yes, Ruth's redirection from anger to humility has come up again and again. Chuck wrenched his back yesterday while bending to plant yellow lilies in front of our wooden fence, and can barely move this morning. Corseted in a black back brace, he came into our bedroom after breakfast, holding his socks and boots and said, "Could you put these on for me? It hurts too much to bend." So he sat on the bed and I got on my knees, bowing at his feet no less, and put on his shoes and socks, just like I still do for our twins in kindergarten. And it was really a loving moment, such a simple thing, really, but he was so appreciative and moved, and I felt, well, like I was his humble servant.

I saw thirty years ahead when we're both starting to teeter around and rely on each other for physical help. I thought about the saying "Grow old with me, the best is yet to be," and know there's lots of truth in those words, that when our health is compromised we need our partners the most.

And in serving others, there is real joy, as anyone knows who tutors kids in language skills or volunteers in a cancer ward. I served my husband, in a little way this morning, and you know, as small as it was, I was so moved by the expression on his face as I slipped on his socks and tied up his boots. He looked like a grateful little boy. If we love our spouses with the same tenderness as we love our children, we could really go places in our marriages.

When my husband feels pampered, he is more affectionate, more positive about me, about us, about everything. And that sets off a cycle of compassion and loving-kindness and passion that keeps going around and around, it does for everyone. That is, until the wheel stops because a husband didn't do something he was supposed to do, and you do everything, so why should you do what has been left undone? You snarl, he snarls back and you're back in the cage, feeling bitter, hateful, not loving, not kind—until you walk into a room and he has surprised you once again, by doing something sweet with the children, or by running the Dustbuster under the kitchen table.

One sure trick for keeping a marriage on track is to let the bitterness pass and not fester, to squash your ego. Push yourself to behave nicely when you feel like throwing things against the wall. Remind yourself how blessed you really are. You're not dying, you're angry. Use the pain.

"In the heart of the fire lies a hidden spring," wrote the Zen master Guin in 1333. Finding the cool water in the heart of the fire is an essential challenge to master in maintaining a marriage. This man does it every day.

Joshua, a Washington attorney, is the father of two sons, ages seventeen and thirteen, who were both born with cerebral palsy. Joshua says that caring for their children has made his relationship with his wife, Nan, a psychotherapist, more real and more unbreakable than most couples he knows.

The son of a Reform rabbi, Joshua never asked himself "Why me?" about the circumstances they have been dealt; in fact, he considers his sharp and funny children as rich and remarkable blessings. Here is the long view of marriage from a husband and father who doesn't sweat the small stuff, doesn't sweat the big stuff, and more than anyone I interviewed gets the full gist of surrendering to marriage.

I've been alive for fifty years and got the shit kicked out of me enough times growing up in Brooklyn that I know that everybody has their problems, you, me, all of us. Most people on the surface present this wonderful facade. But when you get to be friends with someone, you go a little below the surface, you find out this person screws around, this one is depressed, this one is narcisstic, this one has a temper, everyone has their stuff. So I don't even think about whether or not I have a perfect marriage. Because when I look around I don't see anything out there I want more.

People ask us all the time what it's like to have disabled children. Whatever problems we have are not based on the fact that our children have handicaps. Problems in our marriage come from what everybody who is married feels—work and stress. But what's unique in our marriage is that when many things go wrong, there is nobody to blame, and we have to work it out.

One of the kids walks with a walker and crutches, the other is in a wheelchair. And because of the kids we have, for Nan and I not to be together isn't really an option. Each day is about surrender, responding to their needs, and yes, giving up a lot of freedom, for both of us. I am tied. This is it. I surrendered a long time ago to the marriage, to the family, and to everything else. But even with having to get our kids dressed and helping them with the bathroom and dozens of other little tasks, when I compare Nan and I to just about every other couple I know, we have one of the strongest relationships.

I'm up four or five times a night because one of my kids will get himself into a certain position, and he can't get himself out of it. It's no one's fault. Usually, when you are frustrated and angry at some of the stuff that happens with kids, your instinct is to bitch at your husband or your wife. But in our situation, for most of the stuff that happens in our house, there is nobody to blame. We have two kids who are at the age where they should be able to take care of themselves. They cannot. We have to be there for them. We should be able to just go out to dinner. We cannot, unless we have a sitter, which is hard to find with our two boys. It has to be someone strong enough to lift them.

My older son, who is seventeen, can't get himself into bed, he can't turn himself over. I do that, it has to be someone strong, he's a big kid now, five-feet-eight, 160 pounds. My other son can't fully undress himself. He can't undo his belt or unbutton his shirt. We do it, and there's no one you can get mad at. And as other people's children become more independent over time and couples gain more independence, we will not, and we never will.

However, we do go out for dinner and get sitters a couple of times a month. We take a week-long vacation each year. Most couples look forward to more time together, and more space, when their kids start driving and we don't have that. And it's not on the horizon. Our oldest son is the one who needs the most help, and maybe he will find a good group home to live in someday; otherwise he'll live with us forever. I don't worry about it. I have developed a very short window of what I'm going to allow myself to worry about.

It changes the whole dynamic of a marriage. Marriage has its highs and lows, but when I hit a low, leaving isn't an option. I couldn't leave Nan with the kids. She is very thin and cannot do the physical work required with the children. As time goes by, there will be less and less she can do physically. And I couldn't imagine living my life without the kids. That's one level. The other level is that I really love Nan.

And, you know, not having the option of leaving is almost better than having an option. When you don't perceive ending your marriage as an option, things in your marriage that may appear too difficult become something you can deal with. People who are very religious take on hardship in their lives by saying, "It's God's will." They don't think about it, they don't go through this big "Why did this happen to me?" And that's how I am about our family. I don't worry about it, I don't regret anything. I know I can never leave, so it's actually easier for me to be married than most people.

It took me years to be comfortable with marriage, however. For most of us self-focused baby boomers, the idea of going from I to we was hard. It's a clipping of the wings. Marriage is all responsibility. Parenting is all responsibility. But I can tell you there's nothing like the rewards I'm getting back from these kids, the most unqualified love I've ever gotten. Marriage is complicated. Being a parent is not. Even with these kids. From the first moment our children were born, they have been very demanding, and very consuming. Perhaps it's been even more difficult for Nan because I think no matter who you are, a mother's identity is always tied up more with her children. And instead of taking the kids to soccer and ballet she takes them to speech therapy and occupational therapy.

I have never seriously in twenty years thought of getting divorced. Nan is my best friend and always has been. I really like her, and I really respect her. We are good roommates. And I'm in a situation with two kids with special needs who I adore, so I

*don't look at raising them as a burden. I was talking to a friend
the other day and he was complaining about his kids and his
marriage, and he said, "Oh, I shouldn't be telling this to you,
you've got it harder." But I told him, "Sounds like you have it a
lot worse than I do."*

*I do not have cerebral palsy and neither does my wife. We
happen to have two great kids who do, bottom line. And when
people pity us, which they never admit to but of course they do,
I don't get it. I mean, we have a solid relationship and two of the
neatest kids in the world.*

When I first heard Joshua talk about his kids I did think,
Oh, this poor man. But as I have gotten to know him over the
years, there is nothing about him that brings on any kind of
pity. He knows exactly who he is and exactly what he has to
do, and that clarity and singlemindedness is an inspiration. I
often think about Joshua saying that when things go wrong in
his family, there is usually nobody to blame. It helps me hold
my tongue when bad stuff happens in our own house, to mop
up the mess myself—be it emotional or physical disarray—
then move on. Here is another story of how good marriages
are capable of bending and flexing to endure challenges. Faced
with her husband's cancer that has rendered him impotent,
Ruby, forty-three, also is discovering the hidden, cool spring
in the heart of the fire. Ruby is a successful New York antiques
dealer who spends several weeks a year scouring Europe for
her shop of French antiques in Soho. Her son, Simon, age five,
is striking and precocious. Her artist husband, Sam, who she
married on New Year's Eve 1990, is also striking and precocious. When I met Sam at a Georgetown garden party in the
summer of 1988, he was the first man I had seen since 1972
who had streaks of blue glitter in his ponytail.

Speaking French and steaming broccoli, they appear to
be the embodiment of the good life; they have fascinating jobs,

a healthy child (who *likes* broccoli), a sizzle to their marriage, an avant-garde life. Yet, close friends know that their circumstances are not charmed. They have weathered two of the biggest setbacks a husband and wife can face, infertility for her, prostate cancer for him. A year after surgery and treatment, Sam, fifty-two, has been declared cancer-free, but he is unable to have an erection naturally. Simon was born after years of drug-induced ovulation cycle, and the last of Sam's stored sperm, banked presurgery, had recently been implanted—to no avail. The previous IVF attempt was successful, but Ruby miscarried after an eleven-week pregnancy.

They are married, gratefully, stoically, unwaveringly. Here is Ruby's take on what having it all, and then some, feels like:

Basically, you are looking at two people who are confident and content in their own skin. We were loved as children and both of our parents stayed together—an important framework. We have clear senses of ourselves, which is great for a marriage, and which has helped us through Sam's cancer.

He is healthy now, he just got back from the doctor, but he still has what he calls "dead dick syndrome." Supposedly they've spared 75 percent of the nerves that run across the prostate, and he can, with Viagra, still have an erection and an orgasm. But it's a whole evening of work; it's not just spontaneous anymore. And, I've gotten really bored of X-rated movies. The doctors think the visual stimulation helps. It's really funny, because our friends will say, "How is he doing?" And I say I'm tired of these awful X-rated movies. And they'll say, "Oh, you have to get the ones done by this British director they're the best"—we're not the only ones watching these films.

The Viagra makes Sam's head really hot, like he has a fever, and he'll often wake up in the middle of the night with a raging headache. But without the Viagra, we don't get much. He's con-

sidering doing these injections that go directly into the penis, and at first he was horrified, but then he realized he has seen me doing hormone injections with huge needles for infertility. And if it's a treatment that's going to work, he is open to it. The doctors say the nerves will regenerate by two years, but it's coming on two years, so I don't know.

It's not the toughest thing in the world, though. The hardest thing has been that we have just had our last chance at another baby. We used up the last of the stored sperm. It has been hard, yes, strange, yes, saying, "I'm not going to have any more children for the rest of my life, and I may not have any regular sex for the rest of my life." Yet, fortunately, I am not the type of person who feels like sex is the most important thing in the world. I don't need sex to feel like I'm a complete person. And Sam's ego is strong enough that he doesn't feel devalued. We have so much. We have our son. What I do need is to feel that my husband loves me, and I do.

Both of us stay physically active and we're both in good shape, and we are healthy, and that is important as well. And, you know, there are other ways of achieving orgasm. In a good marriage, there has got to be a vast subtext there, aside from sex, and we have that. Our relationship works on many levels. In that sense, I think we've been lucky. In fact, I think our relationship is stronger in spite of all this. I do wish at times he would be more self-reflective about this; really, having cancer has not changed the way he looks at life, there is not a deeper sense of immediacy, like some people get. But Sam is there for me, and he knows I am there for him, and that's a big part of making it together in the long term.

Unlike most people we know, Sam doesn't feel an urgency to be achieving all the time. When he was dealing with cancer, his concern was for Simon. A few times he would say: "If I die, what would there be for me to leave my son to remember me by?" So I do think there are times that he reflects on things he *would like to do in his career and has not produced yet. But, really, it hasn't made him do anything differently. Except he does now go to the gym religiously. I have always been the one who has to make most of the money. I have always been the more successful in my career. It has never bothered him, although it does bother me that he doesn't produce more, I admit that. But we both know what really matters.*

In recent years, I find that I get a lot of value out of going to church. We're both Catholic. Church is good at this time in our lives, and it's important for our son. I feel a responsibility to offer our child what we were given—a sense of a larger order in the universe, a sense of morality, and a sense of being grounded in something larger than ourselves. My faith has helped me handle the challenges in marriage.

With my husband, however, even before he was sexually dysfunctional, the level of trust was always there. That's just the way he is. Because when I met him I was dating his very good friend and even though Sam was attracted to me, he never came on to me. I was someone else's girlfriend. Again, I think I'm lucky to have found the right person. It's just a basic respect for each other, and enough of a crossover in our individual rhythms. Even though I'm much more of a doer than he is. But there has always been an elemental trust and respect.

And there was a definite magic there when we began our relationship. There was definitely a very strong love and attraction that has sustained itself through some torturous highs and lows. It was right there for us, right from the beginning, a sense that we were right, and it was right for us to start a family.

Sam is still a huge resource of affection; and the whole reason you want to be with someone is so above and beyond sex. I find him very attractive. I love watching him perform, that's what it's like, when he's having conversations at parties. You know, some couples when they meet each other, sex is wonderful and hot and then when the sex is gone, the relationship is gone.

The sex is all there really was. It's never been like that for us. I have never in all our years together even considered leaving Sam. I'm too practical, and I'm too in love.

And we do have the responsibility of raising our son together. I didn't just have a child on a whim, and I'm not going to opt out of a marriage just because I'm not getting what the outside world might define as 100 percent. The one regret I have for our boy is that he won't have any brothers or sisters. But hopefully he will have that sort of bond with his cousins. And maybe we'll adopt one day. I do not regret much else. No, I don't. My husband is alive and healthy, and I have work that I love, and a son we both love.

Listening to Joshua and Ruby, we come to understand the true meaning of marriage, a promise to stay on board, through sickness, frustration, boredom, the inevitable itch. We make a promise, and we are supposed to keep that promise. Despite their trying circumstances, they both know they are lucky to be with partners who are friends, lovers, coparents, there for the duration. These are relationships that run at a steady hum, not sharp peaks alternated by sharp plunges, the bronco-riding brand of love. My own marriage is at a steady hum these days, an easy gait, no longer a wild horse ride that flings me all over the place.

This past Valentine's Day, Chuck presented me with a sterling silver choker on which are suspended beautiful pieces of beach glass in shell pink and pale turquoise. This glass that was once jagged and sharp has now been worn smooth with the waves, by banging up against rocks, and grating against the sand. In a marriage, two jagged people with sharp edges continually bang up against each other and over time the edges wear smooth, and the two people become molded to each other. It is not perfect, but it is what it is, and what it is ain't so bad. Beats the hell out of what isn't.

What isn't is the stuff of fantasies, the stuff that makes you feel great in your dream, but when it comes alive in real time is wrong, flawed. Fantasies, most of them, are well, fantastic; why not leave them as that? Fantasy is intoxicating. It doesn't hurt anyone. It doesn't destroy families. It's a spiritual dimension of our humanity that enriches us, it gives us a link to the mystical and the magical that we don't find in the ordinary grind. Yet, the ordinary can be extraordinarily soothing.

Last month we went to Chicago for my niece Talia's bat mitzvah and at the hotel on Sunday morning my husband ran out to a nearby Dunkin Donuts to buy us some coffee and a dozen doughnuts because it was too early for room service. The four boys were in one king-size bed and Chuck came back with a pink-and-white box bulging with frosted treats, some vanilla, some chocolate, some honey-glazed. The boys each grabbed two, I put washcloths down in front of them, and as they stuffed them in their mouths, smears of chocolate now on the sheets and their cheeks, my husband said: "Donuts in bed on a Sunday morning. It doesn't get any better than this."

It doesn't get much better than this. The older I get the more sure I become that the peaks and passing fancies are not what ultimately make for happiness. I can't say that the grind of the ordinary makes me happy, either, day in and day out. But living out a conventional marriage with children and a husband has forced me to know that happiness is only ours in fragments, in delicious bites that we need to thoroughly savor, because, hey, the next day could be a whole different story. Can any human ever really be happy? The answer is yes. The answer is no. The answer is sometimes.

I am seated in the home basement office of Dr. Isaiah Zimmerman, seventy-one, a Washington psychologist who has been working with couples for nearly half of a century. He is tall and white-haired and wears gold-rimmed glasses. Zimmerman's fees—$250 an hour—are among the highest in town, yet people pay willingly because he has a reputation for being the last stop to make when a marriage is on the brink and a real choice needs to be made.

Clients can safely vent their most seething of emotions in Zimmerman's office, a quiet space shielded from the world by two padded, solid wood doors. The pain he witnesses as a relationship specialist is a pain he has felt himself; Zimmerman is divorced from the mother of his three children and in a second marriage. Here are his thoughts on the evolving institution of marriage after nearly five decades on the fifty-yard line, with clients that largely range from middle-class to upper-income groups.

Although each couple is unique, there are a few recurring themes. One that is very strong in the baby boom generation is the belief that you can have it all. That you can somehow have a super-jumbo-size life just like you have enormous, fat cars and fat houses with enormous TVs, and you are eating enormous triple cheeseburgers at McDonald's, and drinking sixty-four-ounce drinks, you know, the Big Gulps, from 7-Eleven.

You expect to have it all in your marriage, too. You believe that you can have exciting sex and tremendous excitement all your life, and if your spouse does not provide it, then you are entitled to have it somewhere else. Beneath the feeling of entitlement, there lies a lot of anger, too, because everything you want actually is impossible to get. And that may lead to separation and divorce. Both men and women can get frustrated, angry, and you give your spouse a deadline: Either you get your act together and give me the passion, attention, and a great sex life, or I'll have to leave you. Sex is a frequent theme in my office, but I would say money often beats it.

I was seeing a couple in their early thirties, both professionals, and they decide to have children. The wife quits her job and stays home with the child. There immediately emerges a power struggle over money. She felt that she could continue being equally responsible for expenditures as she had in the past. And he felt that as he was now the sole breadwinner and their income had dropped significantly, that he was the boss, since it was his sweat putting the bread on the table. That's fairly typical.

Then they started fighting over all sorts of expenses, large and small, and each also felt the partner was unreasonable and tyrannical. The problem was cleared up gradually when I provoked them to look at their feelings of entitlement to their previous level of material expectations, and how they felt they should continue living at that level despite the loss of one paycheck. They were absolutely blind to this. Then I helped them become aware of how lonely their life had become; she was drowned in childcare and he was drowned in his business. At the end of the day, they were exhausted and unsympathetic to each other. We worked out ways they could become partners again; I actually sat down with them and worked out a budget, which I've done with other couples. It's not something therapists generally do, but I do it because money is a problem that can bring up a lot of other hidden problems.

Sex is different because it identifies people as being young forever. Having a wonderful sex life means to a man that he is virile; not necessarily that your body is young, but you yourself are young. When you are having good sex, you naturally feel attractive, people flirt with you, you feel socially desirable. The woman feels, "I'm a great lay." The man feels, "I'm a great stud." And no one gets that all the time from a spouse, so you end up feeling that marriage has failed you, and you may keep finding fault with your spouse. They rarely find fault with themselves.

Of course, men and women have a different approach to sex; men are more fantasy filled. Men accept that sex is a fantasy of theirs which periodically can be fulfilled by a certain woman, but also can be easily fulfilled by masturbating or ogling a center fold. Women are quite different. Obviously women also have fantasy lives, but they tend to seek in the fantasy a reliable relationship that includes good sex. But the most important element is finding someone who is very interested in her, in her thoughts, in her feelings and is sensitive to her moods.

The most common complaint I hear from a woman is that her husband does not communicate. That "the husband isn't interested in me and in what's going on inside me. He doesn't inquire about my inner life." Women like to be talked to, looked into, by their men. And what I do a lot with husbands, those who are reachable, is teach them to take a longer time to make love, to take a longer time being curious and listening to your wife's inner world. And that makes a tremendous difference. That is one of the real secrets that can improve a marriage dramatically. Sadly, not many men are able to get that message.

I hear a lot from couples that their sex is not passionate. It's pleasant. It's like contractual sex to reassure ourselves that "we are still a couple, that we still love each other." Yet, tepid sex is not necessarily what you should expect down the road. There are stages, which includes transformative sex, and at each stage the marriage has to be worked through. If you don't work it through you'll be stuck at a tepid level, not only tepid sex but a tepid quality of life.

You have to be open to change, sexually and in reference to each other's inner world. Let's say the husband wants the wife to dress up in sexually provocative attire. To many women, sexual attire means a beautiful negligee. But for many men, it could mean a get-up reminiscent of a go-go girl or a stripper. Many wives couldn't bring themselves to do this, they don't feel comfortable, refuse, discussion stops, and the subject is buried. Then the husband will often turn to the Internet late at night, looking at pornography and masturbating. Sometimes after the wife is asleep, a husband might postpone his satisfaction until he gets *into bed right next to his wife, he imagines her in long, black stockings, high heels and a garter belt and satisfies himself with that kind of image. But poignantly, he does this while he is right next to her, and she is asleep.*

A breakthrough with such a couple came after I enabled them to be more serious and respectful of each other's quite different sensual needs and images. You can't get good sex without first working through your anger. Anger is the closed door to good sex.

Anger is based on expecting good, easy, natural sex, that your partner will read your mind and just do whatever specifically turns you on. It took several months of work with this couple; he had developed a secret sex life on the Internet, and had gotten into chat rooms to talk dirty to someone who was anonymous. In the meantime, the wife felt he was disinterested in her. She was appalled that the very man who used to be aroused just looking at her now needed her to get dressed up like a stripper to become aroused. She felt it was demeaning and insulting.

She said that she wasn't going to cater to his childishness. And so this was a terrible impasse, an impasse that exists in many tepid marriages. He is disappointed that his fantasies are not being fulfilled, she is disappointed because her expectations of her lifelong attractiveness to her husband isn't being fulfilled. And we did finally work through the anger in our sessions; they started telling each other what their wishes were. And I cautioned them that their wishes would not necessarily be fulfilled but they can appreciate getting to know each other, finally, after twenty years of marriage. Her wish is for a romantic, caring, aroused husband. And his wish is for a sexually enticing, dressed-up woman.

They eventually compromised and they became vulnerable and understanding about their disappointments. It takes an enormous amount of work to get through this anger, but when you do it, the compassion comes through, then the tears, then the understanding; then the empathy.

What they evolved into was not the sex they had when they were a young couple, but the sex of a mature couple who understood each other's wishes, and started catering to some of those wishes—in terms of fantasy talk, dressing up sometimes, not dressing up other times. They started developing a wider range of sexual life that included separate pleasure for him and different pleasure for her.

When there is a lot of anger that has been left alone, it's not unusual for people to come in and have only slept together once a year, or once every two years and so forth. It's embarrassing, and people don't like to talk about it. But it is possible to turn that around if you get through the resentment, and start developing real intimacy by talking to each other and learning about each other's different needs.

I believe there are three concepts upon which a good marriage rests. One, you have to be curious about each other; you have to really be actively interested in each other's inner life. Two, you have to remember this inner life in all its complexity; that is, recall and retain what you know about your partner's inner life, which includes sexual fantasies, career wishes, money wishes, lifestyle, friends, clothes, family. Three, you must consciously apply this to the betterment of the marriage, and this can create a very good partnership.

When I started doing marriage therapy in the late 1950s and early 1960s, the goals were different. More couples came in to hold their marriage together and not hurt the kids, but they did not necessarily want to raise the quality of their relationship. Today, the quality of the relationship seems to come first to most; they want to have a satisfaction on many fronts and they are very demanding of their partners. And if it doesn't work, people are not embarrassed about divorce. They do not feel it to be a horrible stigma. What is also different today is that they want

quality but, paradoxically, they want to enjoy it in very com-
pacted time frames.

People simply feel they have no time. They don't cook, they
carry out. There is no such thing as leisure time. They talk a lot
about quality time, but it turns out in most cases, people actually
spend pathetically little time together. Many couples remark,
sadly, that the most time they spend together, talking or listening,
is in my office. My office is sort of like an intimacy motel.

Many people are lonely in their marriages; it has always
been a primary problem, but women voice it more. The malaise
of the 1950s woman and the 1960s woman, not unlike now, was
that the husband was not paying attention to her. Either he was
away working or in the basement with his tools. And the woman
was confined to the kitchen and to cleaning the house and to
caring for the children. She played the part of happy wife, yet she
was not feeling connected or fulfilled, and she didn't have the
concepts of feminism yet to express her dissatisfaction. At that
time, the notion of having it all, that a woman is entitled to good
sex, a great career, and a fulfilling motherhood, was not widely
held.

During the 1960s, there was an evolution, with the destruc-
tion of many limits. People became more openly interested in
kinky sex, group sex, and open marriages; the point was to pursue
an individually designed and fulfilling private life. Everything
was me, me, me, and the kind of society people wanted was one
with wide liberties, politically and socially. In going from the
fifties to the sixties, my work at that time felt very much like
anthropological cross-cultural work. Yet my focus remained
steering couples toward paying attention to each other's inner
lives, having more realistic expectations, and dealing with anger
that is generally based on frustrated entitlement.

Looking back at the 1960s, there was much more of a spiritual and political ideal to fulfill yourself, rather than seeking fulfillment as a couple. However in the 1980s and 1990s, we entered

into an era where we want to be fulfilled as a couple more than as individuals. I see this as an improvement over the self-centeredness of the sixties. So we have an interesting paradox—while people sincerely want to be fulfilled as a couple, they each feel very entitled to a life that has it all, and therefore hold each other totally responsible for the fulfillment of the marriage.

When a couple first comes to me, I try not to speculate whether this marriage is doomed or not. I believe that if they are willing to come in and at least look at something in the relationship, there is a possibility that some angle of our work could bring success. Even when people say they are in love with someone else, I keep working with them to be curious and alive to the partner they are married to, to learn about them.

Usually the same thing is happening in the affair; they're not really getting to know each other, and they are often dealing with anger carried over from the marriage, and anger forming in the secret relationship itself. Of course, it is always possible that an affair does turn into a love-of-your-life situation, but I do not see that happening often. Largely, affairs are fantasies that fizzle out; they go through the same phases a marriage does, only quicker and with no societal support. I would hazard to guess that about a third of my patients have had affairs, and it is a little bit more men than women, although women are having more affairs than they used to.

With women, it is more typical that the outside relationship is more emotional than sexual, the satisfaction is that this man is paying exquisite attention to them. Men are much more externally oriented and want a Penthouse magazine thrill.

After the initial excitement phase is over in an affair, then comes the turmoil that someone is giving the other less and less time and paying less and less attention, just like in marriage. So the affair gets cut back drastically and someone starts complaining that the other is not available and not delivering what each feels entitled to. This is a time when a person may start appreci-

ating their husband or wife more. But there are some people who will start at this time looking for a new lover; men are more prone to serial affairs. Women are still looking for the love of their life rather than a series of lovers.

There are many stories I have heard that might seem strange. People's private lives are so varied and extraordinary when you can get closer to the truth. One woman whose husband was compulsively having affairs initiated the pathetic ritual of taking a ballpoint pen and making a mark on the head of his penis, which he agreed to, with the assumption being that if he made love during the day it would rub off. On his return home she would examine him. After a while, I got them to question their behavior.

At the heart of most problems is anger that you aren't getting what you think you are entitled to. So anger needs to be addressed and worked through. You know, I've had a marriage that did not work, so really, I'm not that much different than my clients. I had to go through a lot of disillusionment and mistakes, and I'm a veteran of individual and psychoanalytical therapy, group therapy, and couples therapy. I spent five days a week for five years on an analytic couch. I've been a client of my own profession.

I was married for the first time for twenty-four years, and we have three children together, a son and two daughters, one grandchild and one on the way. I feel that I can empathize with my clients because I've been in similar trouble. I have been just as stupid, just as blind, just as impulsive. My first wife and I did not have enough patience in thoughtfully and curiously unraveling each other's inner life. To be interested in each other takes hard work and a great deal of time. Unfortunately, most people would rather avoid the inner world and focus on the outer world, with its seductions.

When I look at the evolution of marriage and think ahead, I am reminded of Margaret Mead's prophetic words that the fu-

ture lies in sequential monogamy. I feel that we will see more situations in which couples feel they cannot mature any more with one partner, they will move on to another marriage to continue their maturation with a new person. That could very well be the model in the future.

I'm talking to Mimi Barash Coppersmith Fredman, a woman whose sequential monogamy was not intentional, yet who exemplifies the Margaret Mead model that it takes more than one partner to fulfill changing needs in the life cycle. Mimi is now on a third marriage; her first two husbands died. She was first married for twenty-one years to Sy Barash, a marriage that produced two daughters. Raised by European immigrant parents in Kingston, Pennsylvania, in a home where sex wasn't discussed, Mimi feels that she was "not as good a partner in my first marriage as I have been in my second and third," because of barriers she had to physical intimacy.

"In my first marriage, I was confused. I hadn't learned the significance of really giving to a partner," she says of Barash, who died of cancer in 1975. "I wasn't open to grow sexually with my first husband. I had headaches. I didn't want to mess my hair. I was too tired. Really, what was going on is that I was inhibited. Sy and I were not unhappy; I just was closed off in a way you shouldn't be in marriage."

Although she grieved deeply, Mimi says she's not the type of person who is particularly good at being alone. One day, as she tells it, she woke up and decided it was time to find another man. "As horrible as that sounds, I did find a gem," says Mimi, of Lou Coppersmith. "Tall, brilliant, handsome, nice." She was forty-three, he was forty-eight, and they married in 1978.

With this husband, her intimacy issues were resolved, as he showed her that sex could be emancipating. "Lou taught me how to really enjoy good sex, and that truly distinguished this as a great love. He made it easy for me to get rid of my inhibitions. He was a great lover, and an incredible person. I am so fortunate to have known that in my life; I know that many people never find it."

In January 1989, Coppersmith went for his daily jog, had a massive heart attack, and never came home. This stunning loss was "beyond description," recalls Mimi. But a fighter and no stranger to death—along with two husbands dying, a brother was also killed at war—Mimi poured everything into her growing business, an advertising/publications company based in State College, Pennsylvania. Yet, alone at night and in the mornings, she grew determined again not to live out the rest of her years solo. When she met up with an old friend of her first husband's, New York Supreme Court Justice Sam Fredman, they were two people who had suffered severe tragedies, and two people who loved to love. Fredman's wife of forty-two years had recently been killed in a car accident, while driving with him in Denmark.

Bonded by their shared grief and long history, Mimi became his second wife and he became her third husband in February of 1990. She said she knew Fredman was the man she should be committing to at this stage of life when soon after the start of their courtship she discovered a malignant lump in her breast and he stuck by her. As she puts it, he told her: "I still want you, Mimi."

Mimi Barash Coppersmith Fredman says her third marriage is about trying to slow down, to spend more time with each of their grandchildren, to cherish the moment together, no simple task for spouses with careers based in two different states. Yet, being immersed in her business is one of the primary reasons Mimi feels she had two successful marriages, and is now having a third one, as well.

"We are fully alive when we're together, and fully alive

when we are apart. That way, as partners, we are never dull to each other. There is always something to talk about."

I'm thinking about Isaiah Zimmerman's belief, after decades of watching it occur before his eyes, that staying curious about a partner's inner world can keep relationships vital and keep dullness from settling in. Indeed, when a husband or wife asks us how we are doing—how our day has gone, is there anything wrong, what is right, things beyond the children—it makes us feel as if we are loved and cared for, the reason we got married in the first place.

When I lecture my journalism students on "the art of the interview" to develop profile-writing skills, I stress the importance of forming and asking direct questions, and how exercising compassion, even humor, is the way to excavate good answers from a subject. They are always shocked, initially, that anyone would want to reveal to them anything personal, especially the more famous Washington personalities I urge them to interview, from politics and the media.

I tell them they will be very surprised how willing to talk openly most people will be, even the most famous of folks, if the interviewer is pleasant and comes at them with genuine interest. People love to talk about themselves, and most people never get a chance to. How many husbands and wives, even the senators and TV anchors, do they think have spouses who routinely ask them about their childhood, what their passions are, to describe their parents, their first love, their disappointments, what's most interesting about their jobs?

My students always laugh after this delivery because they flash on their own parents, who are about my age, who come home after a long day of two careers and hardly sit down to talk leisurely, making sure they are amply inquiring about their partner's inner world. Teaching journalism students about the art of getting another person to open up always reminds me that I should take my own advice more often; to keep asking and asking, and not forgetting to ask, about what the hell is going on inside of my husband.

My friend Moe Hanson asked me what I thought of marriage after all this talking and writing about it, and I told her I know four things: A. Marriage can be hell; B. The grass is not greener on the other side; C. Savor the highs, because one thing you can count on—the dips are just around the corner; and D. You may as well love the one you're with—no one is perfect.

Yet obsessing about marriage has put me in a very strange place about marriage, my marriage, everyone's marriage, about marriage itself. Frankly, I know too much. About what can go wrong, about marriages that sound so right that they make you feel sick to your stomach about your own imperfect one. I know about disaster divorces and great remarriages, about couples who succumb to mediocrity so as not to upset the status quo. I know that all these stories and all these feelings should make us feel less alone; everyone wades through some depth of mucky swamp, and everyone must exert a grand, and unrelenting, effort to push forward, despite the currents that try to pull us back.

We know all the clichés; you don't get it all in one place, marriage is what you make it, you take your own baggage wherever you go. And I don't know if I'm willing to surrender to this promise of partial happiness, that sorrow is in the mix as much as joy, that it's never really A-OK. But we have to surrender, we all do; you make your bed and you lie in it, as my mother always said when she was trying to tame me, her wild teenage daughter. I know that crushes and flirting and cavorting may anesthetize the pain, but it's a bandage for something chronic that needs to be addressed, either with a commitment to try again, or by cutting your losses and starting anew with someone else.

Chuck and I are lucky because we do have peaks of hot,

mad love, and although there are cold spells, we won't give up. We have watched too many friends leave warm nests for exotic adventures only to come fluttering home. We know that no matter where they go their new lovers can never be to them what the spouses are—parents to their children. We have seen perfect affairs dissipate in a few short months when a mom and dad who are parenting the same brood begin to live apart. It keeps us going when the going is rough.

LOVE, HATE, AND THE FINE LINE BETWEEN

Diane Sollee is the founder of the Coalition for Marriage, Family, and Couples Education, as well as smartmarriage.com, nerve centers of the swelling marriage-strengthening movement. Sollee spent most of her professional life promoting therapy as a marriage and family therapist and as an executive director at the American Association for Marriage and Family Therapy. Today, she no longer considers therapy to be the answer for troubled relationships.

Instead, she believes in marriage education, convinced that if we get the following information to couples they can change their odds at marital survival. Drinking coffee in her Washington kitchen and flushed from a morning workout, Sollee, fifty-seven, divorced since 1978, talks about the new research and her reasons for optimism in what she calls a "marriage renaissance." She believes the next generation—including her five grandchildren—have every chance to become masters at marriage.

The divorce epidemic was just a part of the times. In the 1960s we began a focus on reform and revolution—on establishing a whole set of individual rights: civil rights, women's rights, reproductive rights, the sexual revolution, equal pay and educa-

tion—and divorce rights. And it's easy when the whole country is focused on individual rights to lose sight of the value of an interdependent, partnership arrangement like marriage.

Now that we've got the individual rights established, we have the luxury of stepping back and realigning the compass. We can now be conscious and purposeful about reassessing where we are with marriage and developing new, more egalitarian models that fit the marriages of a new millennium.

All of marriage therapy's expansion and impact didn't even put a dent in the thirty-year, fifty-percent divorce rate. Part of the problem is that the therapist industry has been just as hip and cool about divorce as the rest of us. It has bent over backward to be neutral about marriage. The prevailing therapeutic attitude has been that if your marriage "isn't working for you," or "if you've fallen out of love," then it probably isn't meant to be and isn't good for you. Or for your kids. You will hear: "Listen to your feelings. Your marriage isn't making you happy, it's making you depressed." Divorce is often approached as a growth experience. The focus and the training are on helping the individuals find happiness. And the view is a very short-term view.

[My organization] Smart Marriages is about telling people it's better to stay married. We help them to take the long view. The biggest news is that you don't have to find the perfect mate— someone with whom you have everything in common and with whom you never disagree. Marriage is two individuals coming together who will perpetually disagree, so if you learn how to manage disagreements, not avoid them and hope they'll resolve themselves, you can have a working marriage—one that will last.

The research is so clear—disagreement is a normal part of a good, sexy marriage! Just knowing that will change the way people approach it. And knowing that there are good ways to disagree and terrible ways, ways that kill off the love, helps people want to find out how to do it right. Despite the terrible odds, people still believe in marriage. Seventy-five percent of those who *divorce run out and marry again. Those people need to switch behaviors, not partners. The research also shows it isn't the people who start out more in love, more committed, more passionate, who have a better shot at a long-term marriage. It's people who have developed the ability to negotiate all of the disagreements that come up every single day.*

There are going to be big disagreements and little disagreements, over lifestyle, parenting, sex, religion, everything. And, as it turns out, you don't need to resolve them. You need to manage them. You need, most of all, to understand each other's positions. To really understand in a way that you could explain every nuance of your partner's stance.

You brought one civilization to a marriage, your husband brought another, and you are creating a new civilization. How can that be easy? On a daily basis, you and your husband are working through hundreds of nuances: How long should we talk? What should we eat? Do we pray? What time do we go to bed? How does money get spent? How should we do holidays? The issues are endless. Then the kids come along. And the reason marital satisfaction often drops after the birth of the first child is because up until this point you were creating a civilization with no members but you. Now it's time for the two of you to get really serious because, now, there are these children involved.

Another crucial skill we have to teach couples is how to handle change, both great big changes and tiny changes. People are terrified of change. But change is inevitable and it's also the fuel, it keeps things from becoming dull. It becomes not "Oh, how boring, I'm married to this same person for the rest of my life," but rather "Wow! Who am I married to today?" You've got to give each other permission to change, to become different people than the ones you married. Really, the opposite of learning how to embrace change and manage disagreements is to divorce. And divorce is not the solution. It doesn't make anyone happy—not in the long run. If divorce was good for anybody, the daddy, the mommy, the big kids, the little kids, I wouldn't be doing the work that I do.

It's real clear what marriage is: It takes a village to raise a child. Well, it takes marriage to make a village. You can't make families or grow people with all this craziness of divorce. Marriage earns you your citizenship papers into a club called adulthood. This whole idea that parents raise children, well, flip it around. Children turn you into adults, really. Marriage allows you to become parents and grandparents for other people. You are creating their story, their history, an entire civilization.

Marriage is a stitch in an intergenerational tapestry—a connection of emotional and financial resources between families and between generations. Break the stitch and the whole tapestry begins to unravel. And the kids lose out. Even in the best of divorces children lose touch with their networks of aunts and uncles, cousins and second cousins, grandparents and great uncles and great aunts, and with their rightful place in the tapestry. They lose access to the encyclopedia of family wisdom that informs them about who they are and what they are part of.

Here's what people who believe that a new marriage is going to make them happier than their old one should know: The most bitter differences and disagreements in remarriage are way too often about the beloved children from our earlier marriages. People make the mistake of thinking divorce is a cure. But marriage isn't a disease. Marriage is a relationship. If you aren't good at relationships, divorce doesn't make you better. You don't leave the doors of divorce court and come out the other side into the Garden of Perpetual Bliss. The sense of freedom and relief is most often short-lived.

Our research tells us that later life is a very happy stage in marriage. We've got the whole honeymoon idea ass-backward. It's not at the beginning when you're trying to figure out how to live with a stranger, and raise small children, and trying to hammer out a civilization. It's after a few decades when you say,

"Look at these kids, look at these grandchildren, look at this re-markable thing that we've done." You are free from the responsi-bility of children, and you do get to be happy, very happy, because you know you have done a good job.

I rarely see people who are happier the second time around in marriage. There's that much more baggage. People who had a very short first marriage that produced no children can very well go on to a happier second marriage. But the statistics on divorce for second marriages where there are children are horrifying; we see a failure rate of upward of 68 percent. You can never really run from the tiger when you break up a family.

A smart marriage is strong—it has deep roots, and lots of healthy foliage. It has staying power. That's why I'm so hopeful about a renaissance. We can teach people what the experts have figured out: marriage is a skill-based relationship and anybody— even all the children and grandchildren of divorce that we've cre-ated—can learn to do it differently. And what you get in return is something we all want. When you are in a good marriage, you get to relax—and so do your kids.

There is a quote from Thornton Wilder's play The Skin of Our Teeth *that has a permanent spot on smartmarriages.com. It should be given to all couples when they marry: "I didn't marry you because you were perfect. I didn't even marry you because I loved you. I married you because you gave me a promise. That promise made up for your faults. And the promise I gave you made up for mine. Two imperfect people got married and it was the promise that made the marriage. And when our children were growing up, it wasn't a house that protected them; and it wasn't our love that protected them—it was that promise."*

I'm looking at our own six-citizen civilization, a word defined in the encyclopedia as "a level of human culture or society characterized by great size and complexity and wide-spread influence." We are not of great size, but our systems, emotional and physical, are complex. I love the notion of our little civilization becoming more populous and cross-pollinating, in many directions.

I'm thinking of the Krasnow-Anthony civilization as my husband and boys eat their dinner, cooked by the wife/ mother—tortillas wrapped around a mixture of refried beans, grated Parmesan, and barbecued chicken. And although watching them eat often makes me never want to eat again, there are also overwhelming feelings that these are my cubs. I take a wet kitchen towel and wipe milk off faces, they squirm loose and flee to the backyard to play catch with lacrosse rackets, followed by their dad. Ours is a grimy and gorgeous civilization, living on a patch of land where deer and fox and our tribe of wild boys roam.

I feel like Wilbur the pig in *Charlotte's Web,* the book by E. B. White my six-year-old son Zane has me read to him over and over. Mourning the death of his friend Charlotte but left with some of her baby spiders to keep him company, the aging Wilbur contemplates his earthy, beautiful world: "It was the best place to be . . . this warm delicious cellar, with the garrulous geese, the changing seasons, the heat of the sun, the passage of swallows, the nearness of rats, the sameness of sheep, the love of spiders, the smell of manure, and the glory of everything."

I am struck at how my children's world, a glorious habitat, is nearly totally formed by me and Chuck, that if we weren't a team, the most basic of systems would disintegrate, systems like food and shelter and consistency. As I write this I'm hearing the clink of toenail clippers and there are four freshly showered boys in a lineup on the grape juice splattered couch waiting for their turn with Chuck, who when he's done will have performed eighty clips, on eight hands and eight feet. Earlier in the day, I clipped two towheads and pulled a tick off one neck. This stage of our civilization reminds me of some chimpanzees I saw at the National Zoo—the mother licking out her baby's ears. The papa was clutching an older sibling and swinging on a rope.

I love this civilization we have created, the glory of everything, and feel a pressing obligation to get it right.

When we choose to have children, we make an elemental commitment to work our marriages to the bone, to give everything we've got. What we get in return is a civilization we created that keeps growing and growing, as an intact and whole organism. What Chuck and I may get are sixteen grandchildren, who have birthday parties we can both attend. What we may get is a golden anniversary trip back to St. Barts, our honeymoon spot, where we will return, worn and weary, but still going at it.

I read wistfully this scene in the book *Isn't It Romantic?* by Barbara Lazear Ascher, in which she described a married couple, Dan and Becky, dancing at the fiftieth birthday party he throws for himself at the Rainbow Room in Rockefeller Center. One of Dan's oldest friends, who has had at least two wives, possibly three, puts his arms around the birthday boy, and weeps as he says: "I'm so happy for you and Becky. I really mean it."

His envious pal reflects in the third person: "At the time it seemed important to say. Knowing all he knows about the pains and turmoil of marriage, about how love can rub you raw and cause you to run from it, he is happy for his friend. He is happy to see that it can work, which is to say that in the end, in intervals, in the blink of an evening, the silky filaments of romance can weave hope back together. . . ."

Hope is indeed what we need to keep going, to put one foot in front of the other, and persevere through the pain and upheaval in marriage. We must carry on, or "swing with it" as my father used to say, when what we really feel like doing is sitting down, crossing our arms, and telling the other person how awful he is.

Deciding you are never really going to leave, but that you are going to agree to disagree, as Diane Sollee suggests, makes the bad times far easier to endure. We know if we swing with it, we're in a movement that is going to take us somewhere else, and it's somewhere better. Fights, even the worst of them, do not last. My arguments with Chuck have gotten shorter and less hostile over time. We actually end up laughing at some point when the bickering becomes absurd. I know what words hurt him the most, and more and more, I'm thinking them rather than saying them.

That is, usually. I'm working on this one: In the dirtiest of battles, I will still occasionally tell my husband, my love, "I hate you." And that just kills him. But I can't help it, I still say it once in a while, and when I do I become again the young girl who said "I hate you" to bullies on Eugene Field playground in Oak Park, punks who shoved on the skating rink or cheated at knock hockey.

Hate is a short and sharp word that cuts to the heart, and it never fails to wound deeply. I say it when I'm feeling so much hurt myself the impulse is to hurt Chuck even more. And he hates when I say it because not only does he not wish to believe that I could actually hate the person I'm married to but he also knows I do it because I realize how much it hurts him. So it's truly an "I gotcha," the arrow that never misses the bull's-eye.

Hate, seething and pure, comes up when you love someone fiercely. If we are passionate about a person, a lover capable of bringing us to the optimal pleasure point of orgasm, this is a person who is also capable of bringing us to a state of optimal rage. When I say "I hate you" to the man I love, what I'm really saying is "I hate that I need you so much. I hate that someone else has made me so vulnerable, so attached."

I'll tell you another thing about hating and rage I learned just recently that can be applied to managing those emotions in a marriage. I was driving at dusk along the dark, narrow, riverfront road that is the fastest route from our house to the Safeway. A red minivan coming at me, too fast and too close, made me swerve off to the side into some bushes. The driver stopped and I rolled down my window about to scream and she headed me off with a simple, "I'm sorry." And it just knocked the hate right out of me. I said, "I'm sorry, too." When I looked up at her I saw that she, too, was also wedged in a grove of bushes, and well, you know, I can't say for sure that it wasn't me who was driving too close and too fast. Really, in most situations that evoke hate, our own behavior was most likely less than loving, too.

When I fight with Chuck, I say I'm sorry as quickly as I can so as not to allow the nastiness to ruin the day. I accept, and expect, feelings of hate to be part of marriage. I am learning how to demonstrate rage silently, to swing with it, because I can count on the hate changing into something wonderful. Just like I can count on tender love turning into badass fighting. Marriage can be a pain, you can count on that. So surrender to that fact and get on with things. When we decide that we are going to stay married, no matter what happens, we do get to relax and our behavior naturally improves over time.

It's no longer "If you do that I'm going to leave"; it's "You can't do that anymore because we're staying together and that behavior isn't acceptable." If you're lucky, the behavior stops. But if you're like most marrieds, no one really changes that much and the only difference in the relationship is that you start tolerating what you used to find intolerable. What happens is we begin to surrender, and this surrender is not a defeat, it's a victory.

How do people stay married? After countless conversations on the topic, I still can't tell you precisely why, but I can tell you I will never stop searching for the answer, nor should you. We have much to learn from people in good marriages, and we need to probe them for advice. I am seated with Chuck on Milissa and Doug's terrace near Spa Creek on a swampy summer night, eating curried grouper and coconut rice. We are five couples, all on first marriages, twelve children among us. Laurie and Jonathan have been together the longest, married twenty-three years; "Sleeping together for thirty," says Jonathan. They met when they were eighteen at a seminar in Seattle that was an offshoot of Werner Erhard's est training. To this day, Laurie and Jonathan still rely on a central mantra from that seminar when obstacles in their relationship arise: "Say what you feel. Say what you want. Say what you're willing to do."

That balmy night with friends, we hardly moved as Laurie spoke about marriage and her staunch belief that to win at the game you need to stick to the rules. Here's more from Laurie, forty-nine, a gregarious saleswoman, who together with her meteorologist husband Jonathan, forty-nine, exhibits an age-defying crackle. Of all the couples I know, their marriage is one of the strongest; she petite, he tall, both with chestnut hair and brown eyes and united in their mission to sustain an intact family for themselves and two children, David, a college sophomore, and Katie, a high school senior.

Her own parents have been married for fifty years, and here's why Laurie feels that she will follow their example:

One of the basic reasons our marriage works is that I never had financial expectations from Jonathan. I went into marriage knowing that I wanted to be an equal earning partner. I have worked most of my marriage, except for the five years I was home with young children. Even then, my mother would send me money for baby-sitters so I could get out of the house with my girlfriends and not always be crazy with the kids.

My mother was an accomplished artist who didn't get paid for her work and I grew up watching her feel beholden to my dad. Her whole identity was dependent on making the meals and entertaining, on her domestic role. She wanted more for me. I have three brothers, and she raised me to have the same career expectations as the males. I also grew up in a home where my parents stayed together, and that was a powerful influence in how I was going to live my own life.

Jonathan's parents split when he was very young, and living through that has helped enormously in how he views marriage. He didn't want to put children through that. From the start, he has been committed to making our marriage work. I set down two rules when we got married. One was that I wanted to live on the East Coast to be near my family. The second was that Jonathan and I were going to be loyal to each other. No open marriage, absolutely none. Not to say the subject hasn't been broached, but it was never a road we went down.

I'm too proud a person to ever stand for that. He knows that. When you go there, the trust is gone. My sister-in-law took my brother back after he had this wild affair, and I love her for doing that, but honestly I could never have done that myself. For me, once you cross the line, there's no turning back. This is not to say that our marriage has always been easy. There have been rough times, and we have watched some of our friends split.

What is very sad to both of us as we watch these divorces is that often these couples are ones that really belong together, you can just feel it, they are perfectly matched. If they had just weathered the storm, they would still be together. Other than the situations of abuse or alcoholism or abandonment, my belief is that you work it out. Children don't deserve to land on the psychologist's couch because of their parents' mistakes.

Frankly, I am really looking forward to the two of us being empty nesters. I see that as a period where we can develop a new relationship beyond the children, and getting back to the place where we can focus on what we have in common other than child raising. I'm looking forward to going to the movies and not worrying about editing an English paper that is due or making sure my vegetarian daughter has enough fruits and vegetables in the house. After thirty years together, I can honestly say I really like my husband. He is an incredible balance for me.

I would miss our friendship terribly if we weren't together. I have never had any urge to flee. None. When we come up against problems, we are usually able to work through them with our old mantra: "Say what you feel. Say what you want. Say what you're willing to do." That worked when we first met and that works today. This is not to say we haven't gone through dry periods in our marriage. When that happens, Jonathan will say, "We need some hotel sex." That means basically we need to get the hell out of the house and be together for three days and remember why we fell in love in the first place.

I look at pictures of us as teenagers, and I remember everything as if it just happened. Jonathan was my first boyfriend, and he's the only man I ever slept with. And since that time I have just held a rock-hard conviction that our relationship is going to weather any storm and go on forever. Maybe it's my Catholic mind-set, but I've set down some rules and stuck by those rules. And I've watched those rules work.

When things are black and white in a marriage, it's so much easier. When you play by the rules, the big problems many people have in marriage just aren't there. We both have the same philosophy on marriage; it's a commitment that you make, and a commitment that you keep. I remember my mother used to tell me these stories about her friends that got divorced. The man would wake up one day, look over at his new young wife next to him in bed, and become very sad when he realized, "What the hell have I done to my family?" Once you have children, you really have to make your marriage work. Kids don't deserve to have your mistakes inflicted upon them.

I'm sitting in my Chevy Suburban talking to Eve, another woman married to her childhood sweetheart, Marc. As our children take a tumbling class together, we're in a parking lot and she's telling me her formula on longevity in love. Eve is thirty-three, a marathon runner, and a prosecutor for the State of Maryland. Her focus is family violence issues and child abuse, an area of law she feels strongly about after enduring years of sexual abuse by her own stepfather. Through her athletic and intellectual victories, Eve has been able to obtain a sense of mastery and control in a life that, as a girl growing up, often felt out of control.

She met Marc when she was fifteen and he was sixteen, while she was working at a clothing store and he came in for a pair of jeans. He turned from an ordinary customer into what she calls "the white knight" who convinced her to tell authorities about her dark secret and begin a life filled with love and light. Here is her story:

I couldn't stop thinking about him, and so some of my friends convinced me to ask him to go to a big event in town. We fell in love that first night. It was April 7, 1984 and I knew after that that I never wanted to be apart from him again in my life. I had this very intense feeling that he knew everything about me, and I knew everything about him, and that we were eternally bonded. And from that moment on, we have never been apart.

It is very strange, really. Immediately, it was this feeling of everything being so right. It seemed that we'd known each other for an eternity. We dated exclusively for the rest of high school, and then he went away to college. His parents did not want us to see each other, and they tried very hard to keep us apart. He comes from a very wealthy family and I didn't, so they didn't believe we belonged together. His father did everything he could to separate us, including having us followed by private detectives, but there was no possible way he was going to separate us.

Soon after we met, I told Marc that my stepfather had sexually abused me much of my childhood. He was the first person I ever told. He was shocked and horrified and really opened my eyes to the fact that I had to escape the sick environment I was living in. My own mother had left my stepfather years earlier, leaving me to live with him alone. So, days after I graduated from high school, Marc was waiting for me when I literally ran away from home at the age of seventeen, complete with jumping out of my bedroom window with garbage bags full of my things. I moved into an apartment with a girlfriend and continued to work retail, and Marc helped me support myself by giving me his daily lunch money. Although I was only seventeen and living on my own without the direction of a parent, I never lost hope because I had Marc.

I started taking classes at the local community college, and eventually joined Marc at the same university. He was the epitome of a knight in shining armor for me. He saved me from the situation I was in, and he elevated me onto a pedestal from day one.

Marc, too, had suffered through a difficult childhood of varying abuses, and, thus, we were kindred spirits, like two leaves blowing in the wind. There was always this feeling of "It's us against them." It took me years of therapy to work through what went on in my home, and, of course, it's not something you ever completely get over. But, eventually, I did get to the point where I reported the abuse to authorities and my stepfather was successfully prosecuted.

Because of what went on in my family, the one area of marital strife we have is that I'm not a touchy-feely, kissy-huggy kind of person. And Marc needs that because he was starved for affection as a child. He never had the kind of warmth that most children enjoy, and he wants that loving touch from his wife. Only it's hard for me to be that person, after what I went

*through. But I'm working on becoming more expressive; it's
something I want to do for him, and for me.*

*For us to have started our relationship so suddenly, intensely
and magically, it's a wonderful place to go back to. It's not like
we both had dozens of other lovers; he is the only lover in my life.
I don't feel like I missed out on anything because even though I
found him in high school, I have in Marc the kind of mate that
everyone spends a lifetime looking for. It's not the overwhelming
sexual desire you feel when you first start dating. It's something
deeper and better; it comes from being with a person who knows
everything about you.*

*What happens in a lot of marriages that don't work is that
the woman loves her children so much she does everything for
them and puts her husband aside. But he's the one who is going
to be there when your kids are grown and gone in not that many
years. And if you haven't done anything in those decades to nurture that relationship, you're going to turn around and that husband is not going to be there, the love will be gone. Marc and I
have grown up together, and grown together. A lot of people in
marriage grow apart, they take different paths. We have always
been on the same path.*

Listening to Eve tell her story of what sounds like near-
perfect love, I'm thinking how each person I spoke to had
their own unique vision of what a good marriage should be
about. Some placed more emphasis on sex, others on camara-
derie. Yet, while comparisons are sure to come up, we cannot
measure our own marital happiness based on someone else's
ideals. When expectations are our own, we will not be disappointed. In Judith Wallerstein's book *The Good Marriage,* she
writes of the diversity among the marriages she studied, all she
considered good:

". . . each of these marriages was a different world, a sov-
ereign country unto itself. Rather than a single archetype of

happy marriage, I found many different kinds. Like a richly detailed tapestry, each relationship was woven from the strands of love, friendship, sexual fulfillment, nurture, protection, emotional security, economic responsibility, and co-parenting. But the patterns in the marital weave varied . . ."

My own interviews show me that what makes a marriage good, really, is that the two people in it are satisfied with the weave, the texture of the tapestry, the varying widths of the strands of sex and friendship, of compassion and passion, of predictability and intrigue. As the institution of marriage evolves with the millennium, the tapestry of what's possible and what's tolerable will only get more intricate, more interesting, more strange. Here are a few more patches from the American marriage quilt: biographies that range from a lesbian marriage to a best-friend marriage to a fairy-tale second marriage. The fabric of each relationship contrasts sharply with the next one, yet the common thread that binds these folks is that they each believe in the power of long-term partnership.

I became interested in committed relationships among gay couples when my son Theo's fourth-grade teacher lent me an exquisite book about the love between two men, *Geography of the Heart* by Fenton Johnson. I knew love and marriage only from the view of a heterosexual woman. But after reading Johnson's memoir, in which he traces his journey from falling in love to losing his partner to AIDS, I was awakened to the fact that there is not gay love and straight love—there is only love.

As Johnson writes of his lover Larry Rose, who died in 1990: "I was beginning to understand the nature of a love so whole that in the end it encompassed everything about ourselves . . . I was beginning to understand how I might love through pain and ugliness, for better or for worse, up to and beyond death. I was beginning to understand how love offers some kind of victory, the thing that enables us to become larger than ourselves, larger than death."

I became curious to interview someone in a gay marriage, and found a couple with two sons, forbidden to marry legally but as married as anyone can get. Jennifer is a tall and tanned veterinarian and has spiky chestnut hair streaked with gray. Dogs are yipping and the smell is sharp and medicinal in her clinic in rural Maryland. Known as Nif, she smiles a dazzling smile as she talks about her boys and her longtime live-in relationship with Cathy, who is Joseph's biological mother by artificial insemination. They adopted a second child, Jack, in Russia.

Although Nif says, "I don't really see my life as any different than anybody else's," her life is different than that of most parents in a partnership. As a lesbian living in Maryland with what the law considers another woman's children, there are no custody rights that protect her, even though she is jointly raising them. If the couple goes their separate ways, the boys will live with Cathy, who is considered their legal guardian. Here are some of the obstacles Nif faces as half of a couple that is not sanctioned by mainstream society, as well as some of the highs she feels are part of a typical marriage:

I'm no different than any other mother who is married with young children. Cathy and I are partners, and these are our boys, and this is our family. The issues that I deal with in my day-to-day life are just like everybody else who has a five-year-old and a seven-year-old. We made a commitment to each other. I wear a ring, she wears a ring, and it's a pretty traditional relationship.

I do feel a sense of permanence with this relationship, and our agreement is that we have to talk about it if we ever felt like we were falling out of love. And I may have an hour or a day where I was mad about something, but I've never felt like I wanted to leave this relationship.

Of course there are times when I wished I could be by my-self, no kids or dogs or phones. And there are special challenges in raising kids as two lesbian women, but I'm really lucky. I own my own business so I don't have to deal with anyone else's opinion on my lifestyle. And this is a small town, and everyone knows us. It's not like they say, "Oh, there goes those two gay girls." And Cathy, before she had Joseph, was a paramedic. So we both are in professions where people in the community looked up to us.

Joseph is seven, and we've always been very open with him about us, although we have not yet had to discuss sex. But it's coming, because he does ask all these questions. He asks us things like, "Are you going to get married to a man someday?" And we say no. At some point, we'll tell him that we are married. But right now, our biggest worry is that he will be made fun of, or treated differently, because his two parents are of the same sex. But we don't try to hide who we are to him, although I don't think any parent wants their child to grow up and be gay. I don't want either one of my sons to be gay. If they are, I would certainly love them. But I would hope that they are not, because I think it's much easier to live in society if you are like the majority of other people.

I am forty-one years old, and I've been gay as long as I've been anything. I was real slow to mature, but I knew I didn't want to be with boys. Then in my twenties, I started dating women. Cathy and I have a major responsibility to our children, I realize that. I don't want them to think we don't like men; you know, that men are bad or that doing male things or being male is bad or wrong. I don't ever want to give them that message directly, or indirectly, and it's been stressful, because you wonder how much of children's behavior they have within them, or they get from their parents. But more and more, I just feel like they are their own people, and we don't have to make them into any-thing. Joseph is excellent in sports, but he likes just as well to sit and color and draw and paint. He likes to play chess. And then there's Jack, who is your very typical little boy. He likes to take his cars and crash them together, and he takes sticks and pretends they are guns. Joseph never did that, and we thought it was because he was around women most of the time. But so is Jack, and he is all boy.

We do have some issues to resolve with the children, but I don't think it's hard to live as same-sex parents raising children. Frankly, I never think about it. The things I think about are how am I going to get to baseball practice and lacrosse practice and get homework done and get to the grocery store and have time to also call my mother.

My commitment is to Cathy, but my commitment is also to be a mother to these children. I can't imagine not living with them and being with them. It would take something drastic for me to make a move. Unfortunately, the law is very screwed up when it comes to rights of gay couples. Fortunately, we both have families that are really, really supportive, very loving toward both of us. Most of the legal problems that I read about are when something happens and the family gets involved, and wants to take the kids. That would never happen in our families.

But if something does happen, the kids will go to Cathy, we know that, and it is very difficult to imagine. She'll say to me sometimes, "I feel stuck," because she knows she couldn't leave even if she wanted to. I have never felt stuck. I could walk out the door. But I have never wanted to. We know other gay couples who have been in relationships more than twenty years. I could see that. I want that. Most of the time, probably all the time, when two women are together for a period of time, they truly are best friends. With heterosexual couples, sometimes they are and sometimes they aren't. If you are best friends, then you've got a really good chance of making it. And we are.

We have everything in common, which is what made us get together in the first place. I was just very attracted to her personality. *What we have going for us is that we're both women and we both want each other to be happy. As far as the sexual plane, we're not like a man and a woman. We are not trying to deal with the sexual issue, which often ends up being a compromise because the way one feels is drastically different than the way the other feels. Between women, attitudes about sex tend to be more the same. I could be really wrong—I've never been in a long term relationship with a man—but I don't think so. Not that you don't have those arguments when one person wants to have sex and one person doesn't. Of course you do.*

I am monogamous, and I wouldn't go for it if my partner was not. Yeah, monogamy to me is the only way to do it. I'm not wanting for much else in this relationship. Cathy is exactly my age, forty-one, born the same month, same year. We grew up in neighboring counties in central Maryland, and when we talk about things we did as a kid, we did the same things, we went to the same places. We both love being a mother. I think the fact that we're such good friends really gives us a shot at going the long haul. And focusing on the good things that happened in a day and not the bad things.

I always knew I wanted kids, even before I met Cathy. But I also knew I wanted to be a veterinarian. And I couldn't see how I could do both. By the time I met her, I was around thirty or so, and I had all but given up on becoming a mother. I didn't want to do it myself, and I hadn't met anybody who I wanted to do it with. And with Cathy, we just knew. We were just high all the time when we met. Of course, the infatuation doesn't last, but you can try to get it back.

What we try to do is try to find a little time here and there for romance. My day off is Thursday, and the boys are in school and that's our day to do something together. In the summer we usually go fishing. In the colder months, we go to lunch. And the children are still young enough that when they go to bed, we have evenings to spend together. We'll go out to a restaurant some-

times and say, "Okay, let's not talk about the kids tonight." But then we eventually start talking about the kids. And it's okay. We both love those kids.

I will never forget going to Russia to get Jack. He was almost two when we adopted him. He was fat, unhealthy fat, all cellulite, no muscle tone, he could hardly walk, he couldn't speak. It was as if he had just been fed and watered and that was it. We picked him from an adoption video.

The woman in the orphanage brought him to us, then stripped him down naked to dress him in the clothing that we had brought. He was crying. I think it was the first time he had ever worn shoes, not slippers. We were scared; we knew no Russian and he knew no English—how were we going to help him calm down and trust us? But an amazing thing happened to him as we left the orphanage. He became a different little boy. He loved the taxi ride, loved looking out the window at the cars and trucks and people and buildings, and he loved his shoes and coat and hat and mittens we had brought for him. To this day he still gets excited over new clothes and especially shoes. It was our first time alone with our new son.

I still get emotional thinking about it. He looked out the window for a while, but it was soon dark and there was nothing more to see. I laid on my back on one of the day beds on the train, Cathy next to me. I just can't imagine not having this partner, this family.

Nif's story is not glamorous. She is married, with children. She takes her sons to sports, struggles to make downtime with her partner, takes out the garbage. She works hard to make a living. But she considers her life "so great," can't imagine it any other way. I remember something couples' counselor Dr. Isaiah Zimmerman told me about the deep friendships that form in enduring relationships as being "the greatest adventure of all." And I am soothed again by the power of the ordinary versus the fleeting joy that comes from chasing one extraordinary experience after the other. Marriage, if it's for the long haul, requires making frequent stops to count the blessings of this moment, this day.

I thought of the perfection of Right Here Right Now when my friend, Sarah, fifty, and recently divorced, came over to commiserate at my kitchen table over the anguish of dating. She had been out nearly every weekend for two months with a promising man. The attraction between them was so intense that they would grope each other's legs under the table at restaurants. Sarah had put off sleeping with him until they knew each other better, and she felt she could trust him. Finally, last Saturday night, they Did It.

Sarah said it was "awesome." But he didn't call the next day, or the next or the next. And now, here it was, nearly a solid week later, and she hadn't heard one word from the jerk.

The grind of marriage may seem like something we want to escape, but like Sarah, those who have escaped and are suddenly free to love whoever and whenever, often find the lack of structure and rules are more scary than revivifying. There is no substitute for knowing that the guy sleeping next to you tonight is going to show up again, night after night.

UNTIL DEATH DO US PART

Roz and Stanley Morrow, who live outside Annapolis, have been together forty-six years. Ample and silver-haired, Roz met the sinewy Stanley one summer long ago when they both worked at the same hotel, the Garden House, in the Catskills. He was the social director, "an older man" of twenty-four. She was the eighteen-year-old staff governess. Four children and seven grandchildren later, they have beat out his recurring cancer and heart ailments and her crippling back problems. Roz, who walks with a steel cane, reiterates Nif's feelings that a marriage that makes it has to have more friendship in the weave than anything else.

Here is her story:

Nothing has changed, really, since the day I met Stan. I never knew him with any hair. He was skinny, and I was a chubby teenager with straight black hair. No way was it love at first sight. We worked together putting together children's shows at this hotel, and I came to know him as kind, good with kids, not overly sexy, just pleasant. After the summer he started to call and he started to visit and we got engaged at the end of the year and married the following September.

Stan, to me, was always as comfortable as an old shoe. That would be advice I would give young people; go for someone comfortable when picking a mate. I was rooming with a girl named June up in the Catskills, and her gentleman friend was one of the waiters and he was French, very sexy, he was always with other women, and he broke her heart. I didn't want any part of a relationship like that. Who needs complicated? Here was Stan; we would sit on the swings and talk about everything under the sun.

You get to know someone very well when you work together every single day for ten weeks. You see each other be kind, and you see each other cranky. You can't put your best face forward for ten straight weeks. And over the years, that's how our marriage has been—honest. We've had a marriage where there has never been a lot of money but there has been a lot of love and fun. After Stan's most recent cancer surgery, we are doing a lot of reflection on the life that we put together. We have friends who matter, our four children and grandchildren who are all close to us, and to each other. And we feel lucky that we are still alive to experience this remarkable life we have put together. Most of my closest friends are still on their first marriages.

I think a lot of people in your generation enter into the relationship knowing that it could be ended in a snap. It makes it tenuous at best; when something really ugly rears its head, the first thought is, I'm out of here, which is really too bad because most things can be worked out if you're patient and willing. When I got married I expected a partner, a friend. Stan is my soul mate, but not in some mystical way. Soul mate means somebody who sees life basically the same way, a kindred spirit, a friend. A woman I knew who finally left her marriage explained her unhappiness to me this way: "When you go out in the world, you pick up your weapons and you stay on your guard. But, when you come home you should be able to park your musket at the front door. But not me, I pick up my weapons when I go in because he is not my best friend. He was never on my side."

Stan is absolutely my best friend. Everybody is faced with different phases in our lives, and a good marriage is with someone who has staying power when the world is crashing. You need someone telling you you're going to come through this. After my back surgery, I didn't know if I'd every walk again. I am walking, with a cane, and Stan encouraged me through this. Stan was my first boyfriend, my first everything, my last boyfriend, and my last everything. I went straight from my mother's house to my marriage house. I see in your generation much more reluctance to really do the hard work it takes in marriage because it's so easy to end it. You can just walk away and start over.

I am sixty-four and Stan is seventy-one and we have always had a long view of marriage. When we married, I didn't love him as much as I came to later on. I married him because he was suitable; he met all of my mother's criteria; my joke is that he walked to the door unaided and we were of the same religion. We were in the same economic bracket, same family backgrounds, same goals.

How important is that sexual component? I never gave it the highest marks. Sex is comfortable, it's part of a marriage, but

it's not the be-all and end-all. The most important things are the
talking and the closeness. Getting married was the easiest thing I
have ever done. I have never looked back.

Leaving Roz and coming home to Chuck, I am very aware
of how physical attractiveness still means so much to me. In
middle age, we both still have hard bodies and healthy sexual
appetites. Roz's story takes us into the last stage of marriage,
into a partnership where the physical component means helping to take care of each other's disintegrating bodies. It will be
a trying phase, a far different place, a definitely unsexy stage
we will all have to accept someday. But death do us part is not
necessarily the last shot at love for the remaining partner, no
matter what age he or she is.

When her husband George died after sixty-one years of
marriage, Alma was certain she'd spend the rest of her life a
lonely widow. But then came Bob, who made her a bride at
eighty-one. I chose her story because it's a telescope into
something that could happen to any one of us, a new, great
love that follows an old, great love.

Drinking vodka on the rocks with a twist of lemon, Alma
talks about what it feels like to be newlywed in a relationship
"where we can't seem to keep our hands off of each other."
Although she has trouble walking now from foot problems
stemming from wearing high heels her whole life, Alma is anything but feeble. A lifelong southern California girl, she dresses
only in pastels, and "anything that sparkles"—her uniform
includes big, silver clip-on earrings, lots of bangle bracelets,
metallic sandals, and glisteny lipstick the color of cotton
candy. She recently bought a sleek six-cylinder Honda, in sil-
very lavender, the same color as her hair.

Alma lives in Hemet, the other side of the mountain from
Palm Springs, and last year she entered the Mrs. Senior Hemet
Beauty Pageant, which the small town holds every year. She

came in runner-up; "The reason I didn't win is because I wore a short cocktail dress for the competition, rather than a long formal," explains Alma. After six decades with George, here's what it feels like to be with Bob, who she married in June of 1998:

Bob is only seventy-five; I married a younger man! It was the last thing I expected to happen. I hadn't been out on a date in what, more than sixty years? But I told him "yes" when he asked me out, and when he knocked on the door, I took one look at Bob and he took one look at me, and the chemistry was there. We just knew it right away. In three months time, we were married.

He was good-looking, clean, he was full of life, a big smile on his face. He had been single for five years, since his wife died. He waited two years, then he dated about thirty-two gals, everyone he knew. But he'd take these gals out to eat, and that would be the end of it, no attraction, no nothing. Then he met me.

That first date, after dinner, we came to my house and I made him a drink. He never made a move; he was very gentlemanly. When he left, I only got a little peck on the cheek.

When I first met Bob, I'd been married for so many years, I was a little leery, naturally, to be with someone else. I married George at age eighteen, almost nineteen, and stayed married for sixty-one years. I lost my mother when I was seven years old, and I grew up being shoved from family to family. I came to like older men because they were more mature, and I needed that. George was eleven years older than me.

Oh, I loved George, we had a wonderful relationship. He was a good worker and he never strayed. As a matter of fact, when I gave birth to my daughter at the beginning of World War II, [he was drafted] and he was classified as A-1. I was so happy, because I knew if something happened to him I'd still always have part of him. But he was kept in the United States, building airplanes.

During the last few years of George's life, he couldn't see very well, he was getting sicker and sicker. He couldn't read or watch TV, he couldn't exercise at all. His body was just withering away. George was ninety-two when he passed away. I had made him a promise that I wouldn't put him in a retirement home, and I never did.

And it was frustrating for me because I couldn't go any-where or do anything, I was taking care of him. We couldn't go out to eat. It was just home, home, home. The only place I could get away to was the grocery store. At the end, George wanted to die. He was in so much misery. To be honest, I was happy for him when he passed away.

I met Bob a short time later, and people thought it was too soon. Even my daughter didn't want me to marry. They said, "Live with him, don't marry him." But I loved him. I knew I had found an honest and stable man.

Bob says that the second time around is better. He loved his wife dearly, but he had to take care of her, too, for five years. And maybe for me, the second time around is better, too. The love seems to be more intense. George was kind of a quiet person, and took things as they came. Bob is exuberant and happy-go-lucky and he shows his love. He's always kissing me. But Bob also loved his wife dearly, and I loved George dearly, and once in a while I call him George and he'll call me Virginia, and we both laugh about it. Yet, this is a different kind of love. I don't know how to express it. It's very romantic. We'll be sitting in the living room and have the stereo on and there will be a song and we'll both be singing it. A lot of our friends who get married the second time, they want to travel all over the world. We're perfectly happy at home, with each other.

I had a very small stroke and couldn't talk for a while. Bob was wonderful during that time. I don't think I'd be here if it wasn't for him. I lost my voice for about four months and had to take speech therapy. We have supported each other through illness; that's what you do when you are married.

I made my first marriage last for sixty-one years, and I'll tell you how. I never went to bed without saying, "I love you." Now, sometimes I didn't mean it because I was mad, but I got it out of my mouth. We always kissed good night. George very seldom got mad, and when he did, I just shut up, I kept still.

What I have found is that, as far as having a lasting marriage, I always put George first and he always put me first. We always wanted the best for each other. Sex is important, too, because sex is a way to show love. But I'm sensible enough to realize now with Bob that we're no spring chickens. I consider our age and our capability, and our relationship is still sexual, but in a different way. Let's say it's a very sexy attraction, but it's not the steamy sex you think of when you're young.

I'm eighty-one years old, I still cuddle with my husband every night, even though we can't do some of the other things. Then I wake him up at 7 a.m. and cuddle some more. Everybody thinks we're lovebirds, we can't keep our hands off each other. Ha! It's nice to have a younger man.

When I met him, I wasn't going to tell him my age. I didn't lie, I just didn't say anything. But he found out. When he proposed to me, I said yes even though I wasn't ready to get married quite that soon. Because he told me, "Well, we don't have that much time left; we have to make every day count." And we got married in the Episcopal church. I wore a pale pink chiffon skirt and a matching beaded top. It is possible to love more than one person deeply.

Don't ever let anyone tell you again that falling in love, complete with innards that do ecstatic flips, is only for the young. The image of Alma, at eighty-one, expectant and girlish, in pink chiffon, makes me know it ain't over until it's over. There are surprises ahead for all of us, at forty-five, sixty-five, eighty-five, until death do us part. David Robinson, sixty-eight, appears totally giddy, like a boy with a corsage tucked behind his back to give to his gal, when he speaks of his new marriage, which came after a wonderful old marriage to a wife who died in February of 1996.

Born in Barton, England, David is the deputy director of the Division of Heart and Vascular Diseases at the National Institutes of Health. He was my professor for several science courses at Georgetown University while I was studying for a master's degree. I watched this portly and jovial man with full white hair and a ruddy complexion grow thinner and pale as his wife of thirty years, Marcia, battled breast cancer. This crushing ordeal, flinging them both between hope and despair as they tried every new clinical drug trial available, left this man with the twinkly blue eyes and quick humor depleted and bereft.

As he supported his wife in her drawn-out illness, Robinson was dealing with his own chronic heart ailment that has required two surgeries. Today, talking to me in his office at NIH, holding a photograph of his new wife who is dressed in blue jean overalls, Robinson jokes that his heart started healing, remarkably, because of this woman, Christine, also from England. They met in the town where they both now live, in the mountains of Shepherdstown, West Virginia, an hour outside of Washington, D.C.

After a swift courtship, they were married July 4, 1998, and Robinson, at sixty-eight, says he still feels like a besotted teenager, in robust health—thanks to a new pacemaker, and a new, powerful love. Here is his story of devastation and resurrection, a transition any one of us could make someday in marriage.

Here we were, both living in this little town in West Virginia. We're both from England, and we had never even known each other.

She had been married before, but had been divorced for fully ten years and built a life for herself in Shepherdstown and was very content. She had no children. Although we both work in Washington, we had settled on Shepherdstown for the same reasons—it is a nice place and people seemed comfortable, and it reminds us of the small towns we're from in England.

We met at a friend's house in September of 1997 and instantly, I just thought she was a wonderful woman, bright, articulate, and clearly the kind of person I would really enjoy. She looked beautiful to me, vitally alive, exciting, you know, her eyes shone like diamonds.

And we clicked in the best way imaginable. Next I invited her to come to my house for tea. And we clicked even further, although she is fifteen years younger than I, so I felt a bit like a crib snatcher. She was fifty when we met. I served the usual little sandwiches, very English, and it was the best tea I have ever laid my hands on.

From that point on, it was as if no matter where we were, we were in each other's back pockets everyday. Things happened immediately, and we were married that July. I knew what I wanted on a permanent basis based on my other marriage—it was a mixture of pure sexual attraction on the one hand, and a sense of excitement about that woman's personality. Someone intellectual, strong. You need a sense that this is a person with whom there's a lot to be shared and an awful lot to be discussed, someone with whom you will be completely open.

When I met Christine, all of those thoughts came flooding in. I'm no believer in the supernatural, but there was this kind of fatal inevitability.

We could have bumped into each other in the bustle of a

supermarket in England, but here we find ourselves together in Shepherdstown. And here I am, nearly two years later, and it is still just as exciting. There's nothing set in concrete, nothing as if we've been together for forty years. It's still new, at every turn.

There is a part of me that wishes we had a long, long time together. That we'd been able to have children together. She would love to have children but never did, and she would have been a wonderful mother. I'm really in love, yes I am. I know this isn't rational, but meeting her was a hit over the head. And I was ready.

It's been twenty-two years since my heart attack, then thirteen years ago I had bypass surgery. So I do have a sense of taking life as it comes to you. And just a couple of months ago, I had a pacemaker put in, I'd been getting dizzy, not enough oxygen being delivered to the brain Let's hope the heart holds up well, because I've got so many blockages in the vessels that support it, I don't think there's any surgeon who would take me on.

I told Christine on one of our first dates that I had some heart trouble. I had to let her know that clearly if I were in her shoes I would ask myself: "Do I want to get involved with a guy who could drop dead in five minutes?" She obviously wanted to go ahead with me. I hadn't been to a cardiologist in eight years, and had just been soldiering on, and one of the things Christine insisted on was to get myself into a doctor's office and let him have a look at me. So I went to see my longtime cardiologist and he said to me: "My God, are you still alive? You look fabulous." And I said the reason I look so good is that I've met this woman and I'm going to marry her. And she has been working on my excess weight and excess eating and excess drinking.

When Marcia died, I started to feel very sorry for myself and that expressed itself in overindulgence in everything. Christine encouraged me to shape up. I virtually hardly touch alcohol these days, and I'm modest in my intake of food. Love does heal.

Love at this age, I can tell you, doesn't feel any different

than love at any age. The physical attraction is still very powerful. There are still episodes of wild jealousy. Christine and her
former husband remained quite friendly. They were in contact
by telephone and visited occasionally. And I didn't want that
bloke around at all. I was in turmoil over it. The kinds of feelings—"What if he gets her back?"—exactly the feelings one
would have at age fifteen. Those same emotions still run rampant.

With Marcia, we had a very happy life. And it was really
quite horrible in the end, when she took almost four years to die
slowly from breast cancer, after trying everything imaginable. She
was one of the first women to have Taxol, and I believe that
Taxol kept her alive eighteen months longer than she would have
been without it.

In our last years, our relationship became stronger, actually.
She realized that she was on the way out. And I knew, too. And
so in those circumstances we were drawn even closer together
because we realized how much we depended on each other. Marcia and I built a relationship that was very large and very loving,
and gave us two tremendous children. Yet, over thirty years, I
don't think Marcia and I got to know each other 100 percent,
which is good, too; you need to be somewhat on the edge. A
certain amount of mystery and complexity is important.

And now I have it again, with Christine, this living on the
edge sort of feeling. What's ahead of us three years from now is
not perfectly predictable. There are great imponderables about
my particular cardiovascular system. Having watched my wife
die, I do know the power of the moment.

Christine and I, we came to each other out of the blue. We
could have been at any age, and the relationship would have
been just the same. And it makes me feel young. I can't believe
when I look at myself in the mirror and I am really sixty-eight. I
don't discern in myself any significant change in the way I ap-

proach things or the way I do things than when I was a young man in my twenties and thirties.

Love feels like love, the way it has always felt. And however much you loved your former wife, you find the second time around there's a real rejuvenation, a real renaissance, in discovering your love for someone else. Christine and I do silly things like leave notes for each other; I have one today in the lunch she made. We're like foolish teenagers.

I felt like a foolish teenager with my husband last night. We got the kids to bed and instead of skewering Chuck about how much sports he watches—how can ice hockey go on for eight months?—I flick off the television, crawl on top of him in his cobalt blue La-Z Boy recliner, and we start making out. It's 9:08 p.m. on a Thursday in June of 2000, and it's still a whole lot of fun to kiss this man I met at a bar called Deja Vu above Georgetown in Washington at around 6:37 p.m. on a Wednesday in October of 1985.

I always thought that first laying eyes on each other at a place named Deja Vu meant something huge, prophetic, a karmic bull's-eye. Because when I met this Chuck who would become my husband, it was as if I had known him forever, that he was an "already been," an "already seen," as the French expression translates into English. It felt like this line from thirteenth-century poet Jaluddin Rumi, known for his mystical verses of love: "Lovers don't finally meet somewhere. They're in each other all along."

Rumi's mystical ecstasy turns into earthly disgust the next night when Chuck is tearing open a bag of Fritos with his teeth, something he always does that I cannot stand and have never been able to change. I launch into my standard routine on why I hate him tearing through plastic wrappers with his incisors: A. It's terrible for your teeth; B. I don't want the boys modeling your behavior; and C. It's totally tacky. Then I ask him something I've never asked: "Why don't you open bottles with your teeth, too?" He tells me that he tried it once, on some champagne, and he chipped a bottom tooth, but hey, that was twenty years ago, and he may try it again. Right now.

The next morning, I'm at my internist's office, early for an appointment. I pick up the new *Redbook*, turning to an interview with Monica Lewinsky. She is talking about marriage, and how despite everything, she is really a traditional woman looking for the perfect mate. Her ideal man, she says, would be someone "smart and very kind, understanding, strong, not physically but emotionally. Someone who will argue with me, but who will also know how to handle me, who can tell me when to shut up and sit down, someone who's got a good sense of humor and wants kids, loves kids." And I just chuckled, really, thinking, that's what we all want going into marriage—we want everything, really. Not only did I want what Lewinsky wanted, but I wanted my man to be physically strong, also; why not get the whole package?

And I got most of it, but there are chunks missing, stuff there I didn't sign on for, pieces I'd like to add on. Nor did Chuck get it all in me, but he got a lot, too much, if you ask him. But even when our marriage feels like it is toppling or exploding, there is always a shatterproof part of me that knows we will make it. Listening to a bounty of voices on marriage and writing these pages, I relate more to the people who say "I could never leave my marriage" than the spouses who have succeeded in breaking free and starting over.

Having parents who stuck together throughout an imperfect relationship certainly has an impact. I have always believed marriage to be a continuum, a point of beginning from which you carry on in an unbroken line. This can't-leave feeling also comes from self-discovery, over a period of decades, through bad mistakes, honest friends, therapy, an honest husband. I am a person who thrives on consistency and structure, someone who believes that building up an accumulated history in the things you value most makes for more happiness than lots of starting and stopping and starting over. I lived in the same house until I went to college. I went to the same summer camp until I was eighteen. Most of my best girlfriends have been the same best girlfriends I've had since childhood. I have taught journalism at American University for going on thirteen years. Since I married Chuck, he gave me four children, a shingled house on a hill, this moment, and a future. If he isn't The One, who else could possibly be?

You plant a seed, the sapling grows into a tree, and that tree grows tallest and most hearty in its home soil—not on foreign terrain. It's the same with human beings; we grow strongest and healthiest from our original roots in the ground from which we sprung, no matter how much we like to try new things, move around, and tinker with our foliage. We are who we are. As my grandmother used to say, an immigrant from Russia: "You can take a horse around the world and it still comes back a horse."

Even when our marriage in those early years felt like it was breaking apart, we always clung together, be it by a strand—but tough was that filament. This is the man who I married, on a blustery night in Chicago. Surrounded by the people we love most, we became wife and husband and dreamed about children. Working at marriage has been a huge, hard deal, monumental. It has taken, is taking, a lot of pain and sweat to get to this place. Why would anyone want to go through this again with someone else?

And so, we are bound, inextricably, working on making it until forever, one hour at a time. I think of all those days when I'd be so upset because Chuck was who he was and he wasn't changing to my vision of who I thought he should be. More demonstrative. Quicker. More urgent. Someone has to be dying for Chuck to think they need a doctor.

I like to analyze, to spin around in convoluted conversation. Chuck sums up his sentiments in two sentences, then moves on. To be honest, I still want him to be different, but what is different about this wanting is that I realize he may never change. And it's okay. Marriage is good, that is, when it's not bad. Over the years, we have softened some of our edges, like the smooth, soft pieces of beach glass that wash up on shore. We both have a growing acceptance, from exhaustion if nothing else, that surrendering to each other in as many ways as possible is easier than sparring about irksome habits that are not going to go away.

For whatever reason, spiritual, sexual, inexplicable, we chose the other and created four children, a civilization with its own heart, its own appendages and purpose, its own indestructibility. Our family is a unified whole, although our partnership of opposites does not always feel whole. The children are the perfect piece of a union that will never be perfect. From my earliest memory, our family unit stabilized me, bolstered me, gave me the courage to take risks because I knew my foundation was solid. I yearn to construct that same sturdy stage for our children, crafted from thick layers of oak, not flimsy plywood. Our children are old enough now to understand that their mother and father may argue, but our combat is more theatrical than threatening, like chest-banging gorillas in the jungle.

Yet, even after the worst of brawls, there has never been a time when I don't get a flutter in my belly as I watch Chuck walking from his purple minivan toward the house, rolled-up architectural drawings under his arm, a big smile breaking when the first of four kids runs toward him. I love this man— that is, when I don't loathe him. The crackle has never died, although its range of intensity goes from cooling embers to a roaring bonfire. During these last few days I listened again to some of the taped interviews of people featured in this book to make sure I extracted all the good stuff from our chats. Over and over I hear stories from husbands and wives who use the words *we don't connect* when talking about their spouses.

This happens to be a week when I am feeling disconnected from my spouse, who is on a deadline for a house under construction, and is coaching two sons on two lacrosse teams nearly every night. I told Chuck I was sad that we never see each other, and that we need to schedule time to be together just like we put lacrosse games on our calendar. Then I got dramatic, telling him that plants wither and die if they don't get sun and water, and so do relationships. Chuck looked and me and said plainly, "So let's go out to dinner." Just like that.

It struck me then, as it has in the past, that it's all in the way we ask. When I come from vulnerability, I get what I want. When I come from snarly anger, the "why don't you ever . . . ?" place, I never get what I want. I learned this lesson again recently, after what was probably the biggest stand-off in our entire marriage, a ten on a one-to-ten scale.

Chuck inherited his family's historic gun collection when his father died, a rare assortment of artillery that includes everything from rifles used in the Civil War by a great-great-great-grandfather to a semiautomatic that belonged to an uncle during his service in Vietnam. When Chuck's mom moved from her home last year, she wanted the guns shifted from her family room to our living room. Chuck grew up hunting and wanted to pass this heritage along, and was excited about having these guns, which he described as "beautiful," on display in our house. I said, "Over my dead body." He said, "It's my house, they are my guns." This escalated into an exchange I don't particularly want to get into here. Suffice it to say, we didn't use our nicest language.

The Anthony family gun collection set off a tortured month of fighting that intensified as moving day for his mother drew closer and she would inquire about when he was going to come over and pick up the guns. Finally I called my mother-in-law and told her that although I knew my father-in-law's wish for Chuck to be the keeper of his guns was a gesture of love, I couldn't have them in our house of four young sons. Then I called Chuck's sister Martha and told her the same thing. The mother of two daughters, Martha said she understood, and that she'd keep the guns. Then I called therapist Ruth, and set up an emergency session.

During this hour, Ruth coached us both into expressing our opposing views without all-out warfare. Chuck talked about how the guns were a part of his father, a part of his childhood, and a legacy of which he wanted his sons to be a part. He said the rule in his family was "that if you shot it you ate it," and talked fondly about having squirrel for dinner. As someone leading community efforts for stricter gun legislation, I talked about my fears for our children, and how I hesitated to even let them play at friends' houses where parents kept guns. Chuck offered to dismantle the guns and keep no ammunition around. I said it was the symbol of the gun itself that was intolerable; that the children had never even been allowed to play with plastic guns. Why would we have the real things around?

I told him that on a scale from one to ten that this was "my ten." Chuck said, "Everything is Iris's ten." Ruth has known us for years, and after listening to the back-and-forth, she got that this *really* was my ten. That I could not budge. That I probably would do what I swore I would do: "I'll throw the guns in the river if they come into the house." And so Chuck, disparagingly, with lots of mean looks in my direction, said he would agree to have the guns kept at his sister's house, as a "temporary solution." I said that temporary may be thirty years; he said, "We'll see." And we will see. All I know is that today, thankfully, the guns are on the other side of the Chesapeake Bay bridge, forty minutes away. The subject still makes us arch our backs, but we came through it—even if those guns remain my ten, and he doesn't get my point.

I am reminded of other, lower-volume clashes when I reach in my closet and grab a shirt and see that there's still a thin, tarry streak on the white wall, a residue from tossed coffee resulting from the argument over whether low-fat foods had more carbohydrates. It makes me laugh, actually, but it is a tentative laugh, because that stain is also a reminder that there is a quiver of darkness to the light of love, that even when things are going great, a fine line divides joy from sorrow.

Last week, Jack, one of our six-year-old twins, was despondent as he shuffled from room to room, trailing his yellow cotton blanket. I said, "What's wrong?" He looked at me with mopey green eyes and said: "Mommy, nothing is perfect." I said, "What do you mean, honey?" And here is what my son told me: "When I go into my bedroom to play with my toys, I want a different toy that is not in there. I wanted to play with Theo, but he was playing with Isaac. I thought we were having macaroni and cheese for dinner but we are having hamburgers." I stared at him, scrunching my forehead, not believing what was coming out of his mouth.

Of course, Jack can't possibly know this yet, but he has uncovered the ancient impediment to sustained happiness. Life is flawed. You want one thing, you get something else. You go to play with a toy, and well, that toy you hoped you'd find is lost. Then when you do find it, it reminds you of another toy you saw advertised on TV, and you want that one instead. Chuck and I like to say the only things we have in common is that we both dislike green peppers, we are both Democrats, and we are attracted to each other. It's not perfect. But, it's a lot. I tell Chuck tonight how lucky I am to be married to him, that he is reliable, sexy, smart, an unbelievable father—what other husband does the weekly grocery shop? He doesn't look up from the Washington Capitals hockey game but mutters: "Wait ten minutes and you'll feel differently."

In about six minutes, I feel differently. Theo has gotten up, says he can't sleep, would I make him some hot chocolate? My son and I walk downstairs to the kitchen but there's no Hershey's cocoa. Chuck forgot to buy any when he went shopping yesterday. I stomp upstairs, stand in front of the television, and demand, "Why didn't you get chocolate powder?" He snaps back, "It wasn't on the list." I then go foraging through the pockets of his pants, pull out a crumbled list, and right in the middle, there it is: "Hershey's mix." I shove it in front of his face and he says: "I'm so stupid. Why don't you do the shopping?" And that shuts me up right away, as it does every time he says it, which he does constantly, because we always have the same fights.

I don't have the patience to pick through sixteen aisles at a Safeway and stuff two carts with $300 worth of purchases for a family of six and Chuck does. So it's his job, not mine. My job is making school lunches at night, slapping together sandwiches in a robotic trance, daydreaming about what was, and what could be, while staying in a marriage I love to question, which keeps it alive, ripe for permanence and possibility.

Back Page from Chuck

Carlos Santana and John McLaughlin had a great album title in 1973, *Love, Devotion, Surrender.* The music was easily forgettable but that title has always resonated with me. For nearly three years as Iris has labored over this book and badgered me for my thoughts—those three words kept coming to mind as the key ingredients of marriage. Love is the attraction, even lust for your partner. That is how it starts. Devotion is a commitment to the other, even when it's not easy or fun. Surrender is the pleasure of understanding the first two.

The "ing" of "surrender*ing*" in the title of both my wife's first and second books is for me her most important life lesson. It's not surrender*ed* in the past tense, as if something's already accomplished; it's not surrend*er*, as in a command that you must do such-and-such. It's surrender*ing*—an unfolding process in the present and into the future. Our marriage is certainly a work-in-progress, as it should be. The sharpness of Iris's profound insights can't always be in focus for either of us—we've got jobs to do, kids to raise, and dozens of other distractions. But those fleeting glimpses of why we're together sustain us, even when we can't stand to be in the same room.

I got you, babe.

Bibliography

Ackerman, Diane. *A Natural History of Love*. New York: Vintage Books, 1995.

Ascher, Barbara Lazear. *Isn't It Romantic*. New York: HarperCollins, 2000.

Boston Women's Health book Collective. *Our Bodies Ourselves*. New York: Simon and Schuster, 1971.

Coontz, Stephanie. *The Way We Never Were: American Families and the Nostalgia Trap*. New York: Basic Books, 2000.

Dalai Lama, Tenzin Gyatso, the Fourteenth. *The Art of Happiness*. New York: Riverhead Books, 1998

De Beauvoir, Simone. *The Second Sex*. New York: Vintage Books, 1990.

Fisher, Helen. *Anatomy of Love*. London: Simon & Schuster, 1992.

Fitch, Noel Riley. *Appetite for Life*. New York: Doubleday, 1999.

Ford, Richard. *Women with Men*. New York: Alfred A. Knopf, 1997.

Frankl, Viktor E. *Man's Search for Meaning*. New York: Washington Square Press, 1985.

Friedan, Betty. *The Feminine Mystique*. New York: Dell Publishing, 1984.

Fromm, Eric. *the Art Of Loving*. New York: Harper & Brothers Publishers, 1956.

Gaffney, Patricia. *The Saving Graces*. New York: Harpercollins, 1999.

Greer, Germaine. *The Female Eunuch*. New York: McGraw-Hill, 1971.

Gyatso, Geshe Kelsang. *Introduction to Buddhism*. London: Tharpa Publications, 1993.

Hendrix, Harville. *Getting the Love You Want*. New York: HarperPerennial, 1990.

Hunt, Morton M., *The Natural History of Love*. New York; Barnes & Noble Books, 1987.

Johnson, Fenton. *Geography of the Heart*. New York: Scribner, 1996.

Johnson, Robert A. *Feminity Lost And Regained*. New York: HarperPerennial, 1990.

240

Jong, Erica. *Fear of Flying.* New York: Signet, 1974.

Joyce, James. *Ulysses.* London: Published for the Egoist Press by John Rodker, Paris, 1922.

Kinsey, Alfred C. *Sexual Behavior in the Human Male.* Philadelphia: W. B. Saunders Co., 1948.

Krasnow, Iris. *Surrendering to Motherhood.* New York: Hyperion, 1997.

Lawrence, D. H. (David Herbert). *Lady Chatterley's Lover.* New York: W. Faro, Inc., 1930.

Markman, Howard. *Fighting for Your Marriage: Positive Steps for Preventing Divorce Preserving a Lasting Love.* San Francisco, Ca.: Jossey-Bass, 1994.

Morgan, Kay Summersby. *Past Forgetting: My love affair with Dwight Eisenhower.* New York: Simon and Schuster, 1976.

Needleman, Jacob. *A Little Book on Love.* New York: Dell Publishing, 1998.

Ovid. *The Art of Love.* Translated by Rolfe Humphries. Bloomington, In.: Indiana University Press, 1957.

Packer, Toni. *The Work of This Moment.* Boston and London: Shambhala, 1990.

Person, Ethel S. *Dreams of Love and Fateful Encounters.* New York: Penguin Books, 1989.

Rumi. *Look! This Is Love, Poems of Rumi.* Trans. by Annemarie Schimmel. Boston and London: Shambhala, 1991.

Salzberg, Sharon. *Loving-Kindness.* Boston and London: Shambhala, 1995.

Stendhal. *Love.* Trans. by Gilbert and Suzanne Sale. Middlesex, England: Penguin Books, 1977.

Stone, Hal and Sidra Winkelman. *Embracing Each Other.* Mill Valley, Calif.: Nataraj, 1989.

Suzuki, Shunryu. *Zen Mind, Beginner's Mind.* New York: Weatherhill, 1970.

Updike, John. *A Month of Sundays.* New York: Ballantine Books, 1996.

Vaughan, James and Peggy. *Beyond Affairs.* Hilton Head Island, SC: Dialog Press, 1980.

Wallerstein, Judith S., and Sandra Blakeslee. *The Good Marriage.* New York: Warner Books, 1996.

Welwood, John. *Love and Awakening.* New York: HarperPerennial, 1997.

White, E. B. (Elwyn Brooks). *Charlotte's Web.* Pictures by Garth Williams. New York: Harper, 1952.

Whitehead, Barbara Dafoe. *The Divorce Culture.* New York: Alfred A. Knopf, 1997.